Understanding Early Years Policy

Second Edition

Understanding Early Years Policy

Second Edition

Peter Baldock, Damien Fitzgerald and Janet Kay

Los Angeles • London • New Delhi • Singapore • Washington DC

©Peter Baldock, Damien Fitzgerald and Janet Kay 2005, 2009
First published 2005
Reprinted 2006 (twice), 2007 (twice)
Second edition published 2009

SAGE Publications Ltd
1 Oliver's Yard
55 City Road
London EC1Y 1SP

SAGE Publications Inc.
2455 Teller Road
Thousand Oaks, California 91320

SAGE Publications India Pvt Ltd
B 1/I 1 Mohan Cooperative Industrial Area
Mathura Road
New Delhi 110 044

SAGE Publications Asia-Pacific Pte Ltd
33 Pekin Street #02–01
Far East Square
Singapore 048763

Library of Congress Control Number: 2008934904

British Library Cataloguing in Publication data

A catalogue record for this book is available from the British
Library

ISBN 978–1-84787–446-7
ISBN 978–1-84787–447-4 (pbk)

Typeset by Dorwyn, Wells, Somerset
Printed in Great Britain by the MPG Books Group

Printed on paper from sustainable resources

Contents

Acknowledgements

We are grateful to Michelle Smith and Mark O'Hara for their valuable comments on an earlier draft of the first edition of the book. We are also grateful to colleagues working in Wales, Scotland and Northern Ireland for their comments on an earlier draft of Chapter 5.

Key for icons

Chapter objectives

Activity

Points for reflection

Case study

Summary

Further reading

About the Authors

Peter Baldock was a teacher and a member of staff at an international organization before spending more than 20 years in community development, always with a particular interest in early years. He has also worked in regulation and inspection and is currently an Associate Tutor for the Open University.

Damien Fitzgerald has worked as a Registered Nurse, teacher and special needs coordinator in early years and primary education and as an LEA support teacher. He is currently a Principal Lecturer at Sheffield Hallam University in Early Childhood and engaged in varied research.

Janet Kay worked as a qualified social worker with children and families for some years before moving into teaching in further and then higher education. She currently works as a Principal Lecturer in Children and Childhood at Sheffield Hallam University.

Preface

Policy has an important impact on the daily life of early years practitioners. Every setting has its own policies. The policies of central and local government establish expectations of those settings and do much to determine their level of resources. All practitioners, but especially those in managerial positions, have to be conscious of these issues. Questions of policy figure significantly on vocational courses, including programmes leading to Early Years Professional Status (EYPS), and others such as those leading to degrees or Foundation Degrees in Early Childhood Studies.

At the same time there are few books available at the moment designed primarily to help students or practitioners negotiate their way around this area. Authors dealing with social policy in general have yet to catch up with the importance now attached to early years services by politicians and the public. There are books and articles that argue for changes in policy, but their objective is at least as much to persuade readers to support those changes as it is to help them understand the process of policy-making. Four years ago we saw the need for a book that would help students and practitioners learn how to understand that process, identify the context in which new policies arise and work out how to influence policy themselves. The first edition of this book was written as a result.

It was not a detailed account of the policies of the government in power at the time we wrote it. Such a reference book would have duplicated information available on the Internet and elsewhere and it would have needed updating on a regular, at least annual, basis to remain accurate. What we tried to do was to explain what policy is and how it comes about in a way that would be relevant for some time to come through any likely changes in detailed policy. We seem to have been successful in this, but changes since we wrote the first edition have suggested the need for this new, updated, edition.

We have used the opportunity of this second edition to make some minor changes and to bring the story up to date. There is, however, one new topic that has been introduced. In the preface to the first edition we acknowledged the fact that, as people who worked in early years in England, we were considering the subject from an English perspective and warned that the reader should assume that it was the situation in England that was being discussed unless we said otherwise quite specifically. Reviewers who were generally kind about the book pointed out that this limited its usefulness. In addition, the process of devolution has not stood still but has developed in many ways that underline the importance of paying specific attention to the rest of the United Kingdom (hereafter UK) outside England. The countries that make up the UK have a great deal in common and, therefore, differences between them on early years policy can provide interesting comparisons that can be used to debate the best way forward in this area. Devolution has also had an impact on policy-making itself – not just adding another tier of decision-making, but also creating a new driving force as each of the three devolved nations attempts to prove itself. As a result of considerations such as these, we have added another chapter that speaks about policy in Wales, Scotland and Northern Ireland.

The book now has seven chapters. Chapter 1 explains what policy is and why it is important. Chapter 2 outlines the development of policy in this field. Chapter 3 describes the factors that influence the development of the aspirations and objectives that constitute basic policy. Chapter 4 describes the process by which aspirations and objectives are translated into specific legislative and administrative measures. Chapter 5 deals with the impact of devolution on policy-making. Chapter 6 looks at the impact of policy on practitioners, children and parents. Chapter 7 deals with the analysis of policy and considers the relevance of different perspectives (of politicians, professionals, parents and children) and the extent to which a coherent early years policy is in the making. Finally, there is a concluding summary. Chapters 1–7 include activities, discussion points or suggestions for reflection designed to help you think further about the issues raised. Chapter 2 also includes a timeline as a summary of developments in the period from 1945 to 2008. The book closes with a list of useful websites and a glossary of terms used as further aids.

The authors owe a debt of gratitude to the students and colleagues with whom we have worked over the last few years and whose questions, observations and comments during discussion have done much to inform what we have said. We remain responsible for the final outcome.

What Is Policy and Why Is It Important?

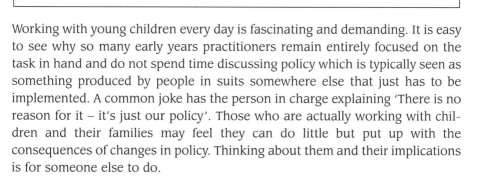

Chapter 1

This chapter explores:

▶ the significant role practitioners play in influencing policy development and implementation

▶ what policy is, examining different meanings of the word, common attributes and why policy is important

▶ three levels of policy-making: the basic assumptions about values and facts that usually underpin policy decisions; the broad objectives; and the detailed arrangements required to meet those objectives

▶ the characteristics of policies

▶ written statements of policy

▶ controversy in the debate on policy.

Working with young children every day is fascinating and demanding. It is easy to see why so many early years practitioners remain entirely focused on the task in hand and do not spend time discussing policy which is typically seen as something produced by people in suits somewhere else that just has to be implemented. A common joke has the person in charge explaining 'There is no reason for it – it's just our policy'. Those who are actually working with children and their families may feel they can do little but put up with the consequences of changes in policy. Thinking about them and their implications is for someone else to do.

This book takes a different approach. We believe that the policies adopted by those in power make an enormous difference to the way practitioners are able to work. We also argue that policies are not just conjured up out of the air. People who make policies have reasons for what they do. We may not agree with them, but they are reasons not mere whims. We need to understand those reasons in order to implement more effectively those policies that appear to be useful and to challenge more effectively those that do not. We want to argue against the sense of helplessness. Practitioners can do more than just cope.

1

Among the sources of policy are what practitioners themselves have to say and they can have a considerable impact on the way that policies are implemented. A good practitioner will give time to think how he/she can help policy develop in useful directions.

What is policy?

Levin (1997) points out that the word 'policy' is used in several different ways and identifies four of these. (The examples given are not from Levin himself, but have been chosen because of their relevance to our overall subject.)

- A stated intention (for example, in 1999 the government announced its intention to transfer responsibility for the regulation of childminding and day care from local authorities to Ofsted – the Office for Standards in Education).

- An action (for example, at quite an early stage it was recognized that there was a strong case for having local Sure Start projects in deprived rural as well as urban areas, and steps were taken to ensure that the overall programme reflected this. Sometimes the word 'policy' is used to cover all the actions the government or some other body has undertaken in a particular field. Thus we speak of 'the government's childcare policy' meaning everything it has done in relation to childcare).

- An organizational or administrative practice (for example, if the government sets up a funding regime for early years settings, there will be policies governing the type of setting that is eligible to receive the money).

- An indication of the formal status of a course of action (policies on, for example, childcare are to be found in documents that have some status, such as a government White Paper or a manifesto published for a general election by a political party).

Although the word does carry different meanings and it is important to be aware of these, there are common elements. Levin says that any policy will denote:

- Belongingness: a policy will belong to some body or another – a political party, a government department, an individual setting, and so on.

- Commitment: a policy entails a commitment to a particular approach or course of action on the part of that body.

- Status: the fact that a proposal or set of ideas is described as a policy suggests that it has been formally adopted in some way by the body that owns it.

- Specificity: a policy will entail specific ways of dealing with specific issues, although the extent to which it is specific on the detail will vary.

These four attributes of policy reflect the fact that policies are considered. People do not usually do things in a completely random way in their everyday lives. The same is also true of policy-makers. We define 'policy' as:

> an attempt by those working inside an organization to think in a coherent way about what it is trying to achieve (either in general or in relation to a specific issue) and what it needs to do to achieve it.

Such thinking is conducted at three levels (although any policy statement may focus on one or two of these):

▸ basic assumptions about the relevant facts and the values that should inform the approach to them.

▸ broad objectives.

▸ detailed arrangements required to meet those objectives.

In many statements of policy the underlying values and statements about what are described as the facts of the situation are presented quite baldly, as though there can be no argument about them. This is because such statements usually come from people in charge and, however much they may have consulted people before issuing the document, they now want to get on with things. It should become clear, in the chapters which follow, that the facts of the situation and the values people bring to bear on them are constantly changing and are often matters of controversy. It is also the case that the distinction between values and facts is far from clear much of the time and people may state as matters of fact things that merely reflect their personal beliefs. In short, we should not take for granted the basic assumptions about values and facts that usually underpin policy decisions even when there is wide consensus on these, perhaps especially when there is consensus.

In the same way, we need to look critically at the second level of policy-making – the broad objectives. Objectives have to be defined clearly, otherwise the policy-makers do not know whether they have been successful and cannot think clearly about further measures their objectives might imply. However, clarity is not always in evidence.

Policy-makers will often argue in favour of a policy on one set of grounds while also having other considerations in mind. For example, both Labour and Conservative governments have often adopted policies that have restricted the powers and autonomy of local councils. There is an inevitable tension between central government, which wishes to set policies for the nation, and local authorities that have to implement policies (especially as the political party controlling a local council may be the opposition party in Parliament). Yet it is difficult to identify a situation where a government has stated explicitly that restricting the autonomy of local government is one of its major aims. Instead they are more likely to talk about policies which have that effect as being designed to secure greater fairness or effectiveness in delivery of services.

Clarity can also be undermined by ambivalence on the part of the policy-makers. For example, a policy designed to give more families access to affordable childcare may be designed to give parents greater freedom of choice or to reduce dependence on benefits (so that it is expected most parents will take up those opportunities). Yet it may be the case that the policy is not described consistently in terms of either of those alternative objectives in spite of the fact that they can be in conflict with each other.

In a large organization, such as the national government, there can also be inconsistency between policies arising from different contexts. For example, at the time of the 2005 general election the Labour Party had policies intended to promote:

▶ the recruitment of more older people into the childcare workforce

▶ the continuing contribution of private providers of day care operating on a small scale (with one or two settings) and of the voluntary and community sector

▶ the development of a better qualified childcare workforce.

At the same time it intended to fund the growing demand for post-16 education among young people partly by depending more on employers for the training of older employees.

A case could be made for each of these policies, but there was a clear tension between them, as discussed further in Chapter 6. Smaller-scale providers (as opposed to local authorities or large commercial organizations) could not afford to fund the training of their older staff or to recruit older staff for whose training they would have to pay. This meant that the developing policy on the funding of post-16 education was restricting the scope for recruiting older people into the childcare workforce and training them. The latest example of this is the Brown government's policy on restricting the funding of courses undertaken by people who already have equivalent or higher qualifications. This will make it much more difficult for graduates to make career switches from their original choices to childcare in middle age. The government of Tony Blair spoke, when it came to power, of wanting to create 'joined-up government', but found this was more difficult in practice than it had anticipated.

The third level of policy-making is that of the detailed arrangements that need to be made if the broad objectives are to be achieved. The law may have to be changed. Organizational structures may have to be put in place. New funding may have to be found. Particular efforts may have to be made to secure support for the broad objectives. Chapter 4 gives many examples of these and other aspects of implementation of policy.

There are always choices to be made in determining what kinds of arrangements will best meet the stated objectives. For example, if it is decided to make it easier for parents to afford childcare, this can be done by:

▸ tax cuts that give parents the means to purchase childcare services, but also give them the freedom to spend the money elsewhere

▸ various forms of tax credit

▸ voucher or grant schemes linked to the purchase of childcare

▸ subsidies paid directly to childcare providers so that they can charge parents less

▸ increased investment in subsidized provision in the public sector (such as local authority day nurseries).

Whichever of these is chosen (and at the time of writing it is still primarily the second and third that are in operation in the UK), the arrangements are likely to be connected with the way in which broad objectives are conceived and with objectives in other fields (such as general economic policy). Policy-makers might also want to offset possible disadvantages in one set of arrangements by creating others without changing the first. For example, the government has sought to prevent the expansion in childcare leading to a decline in the quality of what is on offer by:

▸ giving financial support to training and providing other quality-enhancing measures in the early years field

▸ issuing curriculum guidance, including the guidance on the new Early Years Foundation Stage that came into effect in September 2008

▸ issuing national standards on care

▸ enforcing care and education standards by giving Ofsted regulatory powers in these fields.

So far we have been talking about government policy, but, if policy is the attempt to think coherently about objectives and the means to achieve them, then policy-making is something that will occur at every organizational level.

The politicians in government will have their own policies, but the UK is not a tightly controlled hierarchical organization where the prime minister decides what he wants to happen and everyone does as he wishes. As described in Chapter 3, the policies of the government are heavily influenced by the views of a wide range of organizations as well as the media and the general public. Once policies have been determined, the government is dependent on many different agencies, and, again, the general public, for their successful implementation, as discussed further in Chapter 4. It is also important to bear in mind that in the field of early education and childcare the national government and Parliament have direct responsibility mainly for England and that the devolved regimes in the other parts of the UK now take the lead on this issue in their own countries (as described in Chapter 5).

Different departments of the Civil Service and government agencies such as Ofsted (or Ofted's equivalents in Wales, Scotland and Northern Ireland), will need their own policies to work up the general directions from the politicians into detailed organizational and financial arrangements.

Local authorities and the local primary care trusts of the National Health Service (NHS) will have their own policies for young children. Increasingly they will be expected to cooperate with each other and make their policies compatible with each other's. The Labour Party, since it came to power in 1997, has taken a number of initiatives to achieve this, about which more is said in the next chapter.

Early years settings will have their own policies and procedures on a whole range of practice issues. In some cases the individual setting will be part of a wider organization, such as the education department or one of the national nursery chains, and will have policies common throughout the wider body.

Activity

Take one of the early years policies of the government or of your local authority as an example.

Describe the effects of that policy on any setting with which you are familiar. The policy could be relevant to the general situation of the setting. It could have helped to make the setting more or less financially viable than it would otherwise have been or it could have affected the type of service offered (for example, the age range or the number of children with special needs received). The policy could also have affected daily practice in a variety of ways.

How has the policy come to have those effects? Have they always been what the policy-makers intended?

What are the characteristics of policies?

If a policy is the outcome of an attempt to think clearly and coherently about a particular issue, then it should have certain characteristics:

▶ The underlying assumptions about values and facts will be apparent.

▶ The broad objectives will be clear. It will be obvious who is intended to benefit from the policy and in what way, and objectives will be compatible with each other.

▶ The costs will be known and accepted by those responsible for implementation.

▶ Structural, financial and other arrangements will be made that are best designed to meet those objectives. Resources of all kinds will match the objectives adopted.

▶ The implications for day-to-day practice will be clear or, at least, the basis will be laid for those implications to be determined.

▶ Plans will be in place for communicating the policy and its implications to all those who need to know about it.

▶ The body making the policy will ensure that this particular policy is compatible with other policies on related topics that it has in place.

▶ The implementation of policy will be reviewed periodically in an effective way, so that policy can be modified if necessary.

Of course, many policies fail to meet all of these requirements all of the time. No one is perfect.

To take one example, those outlining a policy may be clear as to the identity of those it is hoped will benefit, but less clear on the identity of those who may be put at a disadvantage (a key part of the costs). Thus it may be understood but not clearly stated that:

▶ tax advantages are being given to families with young children, *but* these will not be shared by other taxpayers

▶ financial assistance with childcare costs must be as simple as possible for parents, *but* this may mean additional paperwork or delays in payment for providers

▶ minimum standards will be required of early years services, *therefore* those unable to reach those standards will be forced to cease operation

▶ services will be required to cooperate more closely to the benefit of users *and* this may mean a loss or renegotiation of professional identity and status for some particular groups of staff.

Of course, the claim will often be made that *in the longer run* the whole of society will benefit from the improvements the policy will bring, so that the short-term disadvantages to some people are acceptable.

Written statements of policy

Policies are normally given a written form. This is not always the case. Custom and practice can govern what is done in the absence of any written policy. Sometimes custom and practice can be more powerful than written policy and take things in a different direction. This is true of central and local government, but is often more obvious in the case of an individual setting. A nursery may have a written policy that there should be close cooperation with parents but undermine that policy by administrative or security practices or the use of professional jargon that have the effect of 'freezing out' parents.

Sometimes practice is not so much about what people do as what they do not do. A kind of negative policy creation can take place. The absence of measures designed to make a setting inclusive and welcoming to children with special needs or from minority cultures can become, in effect, a policy to be exclusive and discriminatory, even though no one would state that that was intended (or, probably, even think it).

Policies should be clear about all the aspects defined in the previous section. Written statements of policy help to achieve this in two ways:

▶ The process of composing a written statement can itself help to clarify ideas that may be shared but not sufficiently articulated or uncover disagreements that had not previously surfaced so that these can be resolved.

▶ A written statement is an essential step in communicating the policy to others (even though it is not usually adequate in itself). The others include, of course, those joining at a later date the body for which the policy was created.

Written policy statements can take three basic forms:

▶ General statements that focus on the underlying assumptions and broad objectives.

▶ Policy statements that spell out those assumptions and objectives in more detailed terms. This might include the identification of issues and possible ways forward on which the policy-makers' views are still tentative and on which they wish to consult.

▶ Detailed statements about the manner in which policy will be implemented.

Written policies are only useful to the extent that reference is made to them on a regular basis and their effectiveness is monitored and reviewed. Again, it may be easier to consider this at the level of the individual setting. Childcare inspectors have sometimes found that settings have excellent sets of written policies and procedures of which the staff seem completely unaware. This is pointless. The important thing is the quality of the experience of the children, not the quality of the document in the manager's office. The procedures are only important to the extent that they are helpful to staff and both govern and reflect their responses to the situations they encounter.

This is why it is dangerous to leave the composition of policy documents to a few experts. If a group of parents new to this kind of thing are trying to set up a pre-school in the local church hall and struggling to raise funds and do the other things they need to do, it may seem helpful if someone from outside offers to produce all their policy documentation for them. In the longer run it can be a recipe for disaster.

Activity

Select a policy statement from a setting in which you are working or have worked (including work as a volunteer or student on placement) and consider the following questions:

- ▶ Have you read the policy statement?
- ▶ Have you received any kind of briefing or training in its implementation?
- ▶ Were you involved in any way in the drafting of the document?
- ▶ Do you understand the reasoning behind the requirements it makes of staff?
- ▶ Are there any changes you would like to see made to the statement? If so, which changes and why?
- ▶ Do you understand what the policy statement requires you to do as a member of staff?
- ▶ Does your ability to understand the policy statement depend on your involvement in developing it?

Controversy in the debate on policy

The next chapter gives an account of the development of government policy up to 2008. Chapter 3 deals with the influences that lead to broad changes in policy, while Chapter 4 explores the ways in which policies are put into practice through changes in the law or administrative arrangements. All three chapters underline some of the problematic aspects of policy. It can be easy to present the development of early years services as something inevitably moving in a single direction, with the main question being how quickly we will get to what is seen as the desired state of affairs. It is a key message of this book that change is a more complex process than that.

In the general election of 2005 all the major parties highlighted early years policy in a way that had not happened before. If anything, the focus on the issue has increased since then.

There are some differences in the approaches adopted by different parties. There are also controversies around issues such as the possible disadvantages of day care, the role of different professions in early years services, the best ways of working with young children to help them benefit from later schooling, the amount of money that needs to go into the early years sector to guarantee quality and whether the state should or should not interfere more in family life.

All of these disputes are important and we will have more to say about some of them in later chapters. However, there are some things that we can confidently expect to continue over the next ten years at least, whichever political party is in government and determining policy:

▶ The expansion of childcare provision will continue, although the expansion is likely to be primarily in the local authority sector or by large national providers in the voluntary and private sectors rather than among community-based groups and childminders operating outside formal networks.

▶ There will be increased attention to the specifics of the early stages of education.

▶ There will be increased investment in the improvement of quality in provision through new emphasis on staff development and training, the developing regulatory systems, the new Foundation Stage curricula and the various kinds of quality assurance scheme.

▶ There will be a new emphasis on family support and other preventive services, providing a different context for attempts to improve measures to safeguard children.

▶ There will be more cross-professional and cross-agency cooperation in the provision of services to children and their parents.

▶ There will be continuing focus on the principle of inclusion in relation to both special needs and cultural diversity.

We can expect these things to happen because the major political parties are in favour of them, whatever differences they may have on points of detail. It can also be anticipated that the development of the European Union (EU) will take things in that direction, although through the influence of what happens in other EU countries rather than any specific EU laws or directives. However, the main reason why things are likely to move in that direction is that they are already doing so and they are doing so at a growing pace because of more fundamental changes in our society in the way in which family life is managed.

Summary

- ▶ There is nothing simple about the subject with which this book deals. However, that is not a reason to run away from policy issues and attempt to concentrate exclusively on the day-to-day job with all its problems and rewards.

- ▶ Policy is important because we have to think about what we are trying to do and why and how we are doing it.

- ▶ The more clearly we think about policy, the better placed we are to implement the policies with which our settings operate.

- ▶ There are opportunities for influencing policy.

- ▶ If we ignore policy issues, they will not go away. With or without our participation, people will make decisions on the organizational context in which early years practitioners operate, the qualifications they need, their pay and other conditions, the resources that will be made available and, above all, what they should be doing with the children day by day.

- ▶ Children need more than our enthusiasm. They need us to think about what we are doing. In the end that is what 'policy' means.

Further reading

The chapters that follow will offer suggestions on further reading on some of the particular topics with which they deal. The field is changing rapidly, but earlier publications are still useful in spelling out some of the general issues and showing how far things have (and have not) moved in the recent past. Among books that can be recommended are:

Penn, H. (ed.) (2000) *Early Childhood Services: Theory, Policy and Practice*, Oxford: Oxford University Press.

Pugh, G. and Duffy, B. (ed.) (2006) *Contemporary Issues in the Early Years: Working Collaboratively for Children* (4th edn), London: Paul Chapman Publishing.

It is also worth looking at early years policy in the context of wider social policy:

Hill, M. (2000) *Understanding Social Policy* (6th edn), London: Blackwell. A standard textbook, although it is worth noting that even the edition produced a couple of years after the general election of 1997 has only a single paragraph reference to early years services, an indication of how long it has taken to recognize the importance of developments since then.

Levin, P. (1997) *Making Social Policy: The Mechanisms of Government and Politics, and How to Investigate Them*, Buckingham: Open University Press. Another useful book quoted earlier in this chapter. Levin is helpful in understanding the complexity of policy-making as a human endeavour, although, again, the book was written too early to reflect the greater priority given to early years by government following the 1997 election.

For those who want to keep up to date on developments in early years policy there are two important sources:

The weekly publication *Nursery World* has useful news items and a lively letters page, and often covers significant policy issues in its longer articles.

The website of the Department for Children, Schools and Families (DCSF) Sure Start Unit (www.surestart.gov.uk) will be an important source of official information, as will the websites of such bodies as your local authority early years team, Sure Start projects, Children's Trust and other bodies which should be easy to track down, but can also be obtained through your local Children's Information Service.

The Development of Early Years Policy So Far

Chapter 2

This chapter considers:

▶ the relevance of changes in attitudes to childhood and early years services to the subject of early years policy

▶ forces that inhibited and encouraged development of early years services from 1939 to 1979

▶ how the issue of early years services grew in importance under Conservative rule (1979–97)

▶ the development of initiatives outside central government

▶ the Labour Party's early years policy, 1997–2001

▶ policy development in the field since 2001.

The broad consensus on the importance of early years services, to which we referred in the last chapter, is new. There were virtually no childcare services until the end of the nineteenth century. It was only in the middle of the twentieth century that governments began to see the care and education of very young children as an area where policy-making was required. This became a question of increasing concern to parents and others in the last third of the twentieth century and forced itself on the attention of government ministers. However, real change did not occur until after the election of the Labour government in 1997 and things have escalated since then. It is important to understand this process of accelerating change in order to prepare for what may come next. At the end of this chapter you will find a timeline that outlines a number of significant developments in early years and their wider context. The purpose of this is to help you understand how policy affecting young children and families has developed over time.

Before the Second World War

Changes in attitudes to early years services reflect changes in attitudes to childhood itself. This is a relatively new area in historical research. It can be traced back to the publication of a book in France in 1960, which claimed that the very idea of childhood was an invention of comparatively recent times (Ariès, 1960). That book inspired a growing body of research that has led to the rejection of the original thesis, but has still confirmed that attitudes to children have gone through many changes in Western society. There is no space here even to outline all the findings of that research, but some key points can be highlighted as having special relevance to the subject of early years policy.

It was, of course, always recognized that very small children needed special care and that slightly older children needed some form of guidance or education to help them take their place in society. However, it was only with the emergence of a larger and more powerful middle class that we began to develop the idea of childhood as a period of life that required its own styles of clothing, dedicated physical spaces, playthings and literature. This started in the seventeenth century, but it was in the nineteenth century that the paraphernalia of childhood became an industry, that working-class as well as middle-class families aspired to provide a protected environment for their children quite separate from the world of work, that novels written for adults began to deal with the (sometimes grim) experiences of children and that books written for children began to show a real appreciation of their tastes and needs. The image of childhood that emerged was often rosy. However, Freud's view that many of the problems of adult life had their roots in childhood experience undermined the idea of childhood innocence that had developed in the previous couple of centuries. The exposure of children to the adult world through advertising and the broadcast media led to changes in, for example, the styles of dress for children. The view that childhood should be a separate golden age remains, nevertheless, very influential in family life and in policy.

While historians have studied childhood, we still do not have a history of early years services. Books dealing with particular aspects of practice, such as Jackson and Jackson (1979) on childminding, Bilton (1998) on outdoor play and Baldock (2001) on regulation, often give some historical background, but the broad picture has yet to be drawn.

Specialist services for young children emerged only very slowly. This was partly because one of the consequences of the moves to protect children in the nineteenth century was the pressure to keep mothers out of the workplace. To the extent that this was successful, it meant that children's day care was not required. Because it was often unsuccessful, cheap, poor quality, entirely unofficial care of children by women known as 'baby-farmers' spread in the industrial cities. Reformers at the end of the nineteenth century and the beginning of the twentieth set up pioneering efforts in nursery education and the provision of outdoor play for the children of the slums. The fact that so much depended on individual initiative meant that the range of services that began to take shape in the first half of the twentieth century was fragmented – with childminding, nursery education, day care and initiatives on play all related to different parts of the developing system of local government.

1939–79: From the Second World War to the election of Margaret Thatcher

Like any emergency, the Second World War led to departures from normal life. Men were drafted into the armed forces. Women, as a result, had to be drafted into industry. It became necessary, therefore, to provide childcare. Local authorities established registers of childminders and set up nurseries. However, these measures were usually seen as exceptional and from the start many voices were heard expressing the wish that large-scale employment of women and provision of day care would disappear once the war was won.

Many nurseries were, indeed, closed down in the late 1940s. The only new initiative of any importance that was taken was to introduce a system for *regulating* childminders and nurseries. That measure came from a moral panic about the dangers of accidental harm to children while they were in the care of people other than their mothers. The emphasis initially was entirely on the prevention of infection or accidental injury.

The concentration on regulation went alongside reductions in state provision, the designation of local authority day care as a way of dealing only with severe family problems and positive discouragement of the employment of mothers of children under three years of age. However, in the course of the 1960s and 1970s a number of things modified this picture.

There was a small increase in the amount of private or voluntary provision. This occurred primarily in middle-class areas and it was only towards the end of the 1970s that the numbers began to grow significantly.

In 1962 the Pre-school Playgroups Association (now the Pre-school Learning Alliance – the PLA) was formed to press for better educational provision for pre-school children. A major part of the organization's strategy was the development of small-scale community-based provision, intended to plug some of the gaps, and show what might be done by the state (Crowe, 1973). Five years after the PLA was formed an influential report on education spoke of the importance of nursery education but refrained from any similar endorsement of day care for young children (DES, 1967).

There were efforts to create more opportunities for outdoor play as worries grew about the amount of time children were spending indoors or their safety when they did venture outdoors on their own. These included adventure playgrounds in the 1960s and holiday playcare schemes (usually run by local authorities) in the 1970s.

The creation of the National Childminding Association (NCMA) gave an effective voice to those who saw positive benefits in a form of care that had a poor image among the general public, and the number of childminders grew.

These were all significant developments, suggesting a more important role for early years services than they were to achieve for some time to come and laying the basis for a more positive policy by the state. When the newly formed social services departments took over regulation of early years services from the old public health departments, perspectives on the purposes of regulation began to alter. The emphasis on physical safety remained, but attention was also paid to social and emotional deprivation, to the ways in which settings could provide a valuable resource to families at risk and to the part regulation could play in protecting children from abuse as well as accidental harm. Unlike those who had managed regulation in the public health departments, many in the social services departments developed a supportive role (to childminders in particular) and some departments appointed specialist advisers to work alongside inspectors.

A handful of local authorities began to establish services that were in some sense or another 'integrated', with education and social services provision taking place on the same sites, Pen Green being the most famous example (Makins, 1997). Managers in education and social services departments who specialized in early years services began to cooperate more closely, a process that neither side found always easy (David, 1994).

A growing number of researchers and practitioners were becoming aware that the fragmented and under-funded early years services in the UK were not part of an inevitable pattern, that in some other countries, especially in Scandinavia, things were done differently, and they began to agitate for similar reforms in this country. The Thomas Coram Foundation, a research body that had strong links with services in other countries, played a particularly strong role in this respect through its research reports and through books, articles and conference papers written by its staff.

Even by the 1970s the pressure for change was feeble. One indication of this was the collapse at the beginning of that decade of the Family Advice Centres set up in the late 1960s (Leissner, 1967; 1972). These centres were similar in scope to the Children's Centres that it is now intended should be provided universally. The collapse was due to the fact that there was no clear plan to make them available across the country. Their failure was a major disappointment to many.

Activity

Study a book or official document dealing with an aspect of early years services that was published before 1979.

> ▶ To what extent are the values and assumptions that underpin the document ones that would be widely accepted today?
>
> ▶ Are there any references or assertions in the text you find puzzling? (If so, can further reading help you understand what was meant?)
>
> ▶ To what extent does the text show an appreciation of the whole early years scene (whether or not it deals with a particular topic)?
>
> ▶ Are the ideas and proposals in the text still valid today?
>
> What have you learned from this exercise about the ways in which attitudes to young children and early years services have changed in the period since the text was published?

1979–97: The years of Conservative rule

The years of Conservative rule from 1979 to 1997 were years in which both forces outlined in the previous section (those that inhibited and those that encouraged the development of early years services) came into increasing conflict within the heart of government itself.

On the one hand, Conservatives talked of a return to Victorian values, of 'getting back to basics'. Measures intended to prevent the alleged 'promotion' of homosexuality in schools and to discourage single parenthood followed. The expansion of childcare to enable mothers of young children to work did not fit easily with this concern for what were often called 'traditional family values'.

On the other hand, the emphasis on self-reliance, the encouragement of home ownership, with the additional family expenditure that could entail, and the example of Margaret Thatcher herself as a married woman with children who reached the peak of success in her own career, all suggested the need to have services that would allow young mothers to return to work. At the same time Sir Keith Joseph, a leading thinker in the Conservative Party (and someone Margaret Thatcher particularly admired), took up the concept of the 'cycle of deprivation' – the idea that inability to cope in the market economy was due to the experiences that children had had when growing up in poverty so that deprivation in one generation laid the basis for deprivation in the next. Among the ways he wanted to break this cycle were the provision of effective education in parenting and better education for pre-school children (Joseph, 1975).

As a result there were several measures designed to support early years services, although these never really amounted to a coherent policy except in so far as practitioners and local politicians made something of any opportunities they offered.

The key measures taken were:

▶ An extended and improved system of regulation for childminding and day care based on Part X of the 1989 Children Act and the guidance issued by the Department of Health to explain its implications (Department of Health, 1991).

▶ Improved systems of child protection built around local child protection procedures and the coordination offered by the Area Child Protection Committees (ACPCs).

▶ The development of the Family Credit system which was intended to assist low-income working parents in ways that would benefit their children.

▶ The invention of the voucher system for nursery education (something that was probably intended as a pilot for the wider use of vouchers in the education system, but which also had the effect of giving further status and income to nurseries and pre-schools).

▶ The work on the 'desirable outcomes for children's learning' (DfEE/SCAA, 1996), the precursor of the later curriculum guidance on the Foundation Stage and, before that, the acceptance in an influential report that pre-school education had to take a different form from that offered in schools (DES, 1990).

When combined with the growing demand for services among sections of the public, these measures encouraged those who wanted to see reform go further. They provided the background for a number of initiatives outside central government. Among these were:

▶ Measures designed to improve the professional development of nursery nurses, childminders and playworkers.

▶ The launching of the Daycare Trust and of a number of new networks of providers, including Kids' Clubs Network (later re-named '4Children').

▶ Initiatives taken by several local authorities, first of all in Strathclyde in Scotland, then in a number of Labour-controlled local authorities in England, to establish 'integrated' services for young children, usually within education departments, bringing together staff from education, social services and sometimes other departments as well.

▶ The publication of books that publicized innovative work taking place looked to examples of good provision in other countries and argued for further reform in practice and institutional arrangements. Examples include Hennessey et al. (1992), David (1994), Goldschmied and Jackson (1994), Smith and Vernon (1994), Pugh (originally published in1996, now Pugh and Duffy, 2006) and Penn (1997).

Early years services were not at the top of the agenda for 'New Labour' when it won the general election of 1997. However, there were hopes that the government would support more enthusiastically and coherently the demands being made by early years professionals, feminists and those concerned with child poverty for a new and improved approach to the issue.

Activity

Talk to someone who was working in an early years setting in the first half of the 1990s, preferably someone still working in the field today.

▶ Ask him/her about the ways in which things have changed since that period. What are the most important of the changes that have taken place?

▶ What is his/her understanding of the thinking behind the changes of which he/she is most aware?

▶ How have the changes he/she has seen impacted on daily practice and on the expectations of parents?

▶ Does he/she see the changes as making things better, on the whole, or worse for practitioners, children and parents?

▶ What do you think of his/her experience?

1997–2001: The Labour Party's return to power

From the start the government of Tony Blair had a positive approach to early years services – an approach that matched to some extent the principles being promoted by the Daycare Trust, the Thomas Coram Foundation and other lobbyists. However, such people frequently expressed impatience with what they saw as the slow pace of change. Moss (2001b) offers an example of this.

The government was wary of making commitments that entailed additional expenditure when, for reasons of financial prudence, it had committed itself to staying initially within spending limits set by the previous government. It was also uncertain how far it could rely on local authorities whose staff it suspected of being too entrenched in their ways. It was nervous of antagonizing the teaching unions by introducing changes that might appear to them to threaten their professional autonomy or increase workloads. All these were among the reasons why it moved slowly at first. The National Childcare Strategy, which it announced soon after taking power, was more ambitious in scope than anything produced by the previous government, but still addressed only part of the overall picture of early years provision. Nevertheless, developments in this period were significant and laid the foundations for the much more coherent policy of their second term after they won the general election of 2001.

Five major elements in the policy were adopted after 1997.

Tackling poverty

The government saw childcare as a key part of an overall strategy for tackling poverty as well as being an important issue in its own right. Their approach needs to be seen in that context. This issue is covered in more detail in Chapter 3.

Promoting partnership

A second element was the promotion of partnership in early years services. 'Partnership' was something of a buzzword in the period. It was already a dominant principle in the design of regeneration programmes in the poorer parts of the country. The new government gave it even more emphasis. Often the word 'partnership' was simply plastered over existing arrangements (such as those for service agreements between local authorities and commercial enterprises). The word was invoked because it sounded cosier than state-controlled provision, on the one hand, or handing welfare provision over to profit-making enterprises on the other. It was part of what the Labour Party was calling the 'Third Way' in politics between socialism and unfettered reliance on the market.

The weaknesses in partnership policy were particularly clear in the early years field. The government asked local authorities to set up Early Years Development and Childcare Partnerships (EYDCPs) in which local authority departments, the NHS, private companies, voluntary organizations and community representatives all had their place. The EYDCPs were given responsibility for the development of services in their areas. The former voucher system was replaced by new nursery grants, a change that implied better planning (but not planning exclusively by the local state) and the replacement of the Conservatives' attempt to create a state-sponsored market in education.

A considerable amount was achieved under the umbrella of the EYDCPs from the time they were formed until 2004 when most of them disappeared as a result of changes in the system for children's services. There were also problems, several of them identified (from central government's perspective) as part of an inter-departmental review of childcare services in general (Strategy Unit, 2002).

The fundamental issue was the extent to which genuine partnership was established. Often the EYDCPs became simply a new mechanism for consultation rather than one for joint planning. Community health services often kept their distance. It proved difficult to establish mechanisms under which people genuinely representative of local parents could take their place on EYDCP boards and most local authorities barely attempted to do this. There were tensions between the independent providers, on the one hand, and local authorities on the other with both sometimes competing for the same four-year-olds in order to secure their financial sustainability. There was the fundamental weakness, to which the Strategy Unit gave special attention, that the EYDCPs were not set up in a way that meant they could be held responsible in law for the way that money was spent, so that significant responsibility and, therefore, power remained with education departments. The experience of the EYDCPs did not undermine the government's commitment to partnership in this field, but it did show that success in this area would depend on a good deal more than setting up bodies with the more obvious interests represented in them.

Encouraging expansion and experiment

The government wanted to see more than the consolidation of existing provision. The third element in its early years policy was the support of expansion and innovation. This was done in a number of ways.

The first was to underpin expansion where it was happening. Funding arrangements set up by the Conservatives for out-of-school care for primary school children were continued and strengthened, while new childcare grants helped to sustain the growth in day-care facilities. One new venture that the government introduced towards the end of this period to which it attached particular importance was the Neighbourhood Nurseries Initiative, a funding programme designed to assist the expansion in the number of full-day care places in poorer areas.

Support was given to initiatives designed to increase professionalism in the early years sector. Examples included the creation of the Council for Awards in Children's Care and Education (CACHE) as a new awarding body, the promotion of playwork education and training and the encouragement given to childminders to join more formally constituted networks under the National Childminding Association (NCMA) umbrella. Again, many of these initiatives had their origins in the period of the previous government, but were now given new impetus.

The Desirable Learning Outcomes and Early Learning Goals were replaced by the *Curriculum Guidance for the Foundation Stage*, which went some way towards strengthening the status of this stage as an important one in its own right (QCA/DfEE, 2000).

Funding was given to settings designated as Early Excellence Centres or as Beacon Schools, not only to assist and encourage them, but also in the hope that they would provide models that could be imitated by others.

A good deal had been achieved by many, especially among community-based nurseries and pre-schools and among nursery schools in the local authority sector, to involve parents and give them additional support. The Sure Start projects were planned to take this a stage further by establishing programmes on a neighbourhood basis rather than on the basis of 'outreach' from day-care or educational settings. The projects suggested ways in which settings could be part of a coherent network of local services – ideas taken up later in the idea of Children's Centres.

The central role given to education

Among those lobbying for better early years services there was agreement that a major weakness of existing provision was its fragmentation. In particular, the division between *care* and *education* in provision and overall planning was seen as artificial and unhelpful. Most felt that education offered the best existing base for early years services. Those who pressed for the creation of an entirely new early years profession offered a more radical perspective (Moss, 2000).

The government moved in the direction of giving an overarching role to education, but did so cautiously. It moved some responsibilities from the Department of Health (which also covered social services), but kept the teams dealing with childcare and early education separate at first in the Department for Education and Employment (DfEE) so that funding regimes remained distinct. The greatest change that was made was in responsibility for the regulation of early years services with the transfer (after the 2001 election but planned and enshrined in law before that) of responsibility from local authorities to Ofsted in England and the Welsh Assembly in Wales.

Better regulation

It would be a caricature to describe early years policy in the period after the Second World War as being one of doing little in the way of service provision and regulating whatever happened to exist. There would, however, be as much truth in it as there can be in any caricature. Regulation was virtually the only positive action promoted by government between 1948 and 1979. Even in the period 1979–97 the reform of regulation under Part X of the 1989 Children Act was probably the single most important thing the government did. The decision to transfer responsibility in England to Ofsted, which was made public in 1999, led to several far-reaching changes in the system of regulation in September 2001 and entailed a major change in the way early years policy was directed at local level.

The key changes in the system set up in England under Ofsted can be summarized as follows:

▶ Separation of regulation from support services for which local authorities were given clear responsibility for the first time.

▶ The opportunity to establish a system of 'combined' inspections, covering both care and education aspects, in those nurseries and pre-schools that were funded as providers of education for three- and four-year-olds and (in the longer term) the possibility of bringing early education within schools and day-care settings under the same inspection regime.

▶ The replacement of 150 local authority services (in England) by a single directorate within Ofsted with the potential for greater consistency in inspection across the country.

▶ The increased opportunities to provide statistical information to government and the public on how different types of setting or different local authorities were performing.

▶ The adoption of National Standards, based on the outcomes expected rather than the very detailed regulation on the measures to be taken, in which many local authorities had engaged and, as a consequence, recognition of the importance of professional responsibility and a more child-focused means of assessing performance.

▶ The opportunity created by the establishment of a new national agency to clarify issues on which there had been some confusion under the previous regime, especially in the area of which services were exempt from registration.

Of all the elements outlined, it is the first that was in many ways the most significant. Registration and inspection units within local authorities had varied considerably in the extent to which they offered support and advice to providers, especially in the process of registration. This was because previous legislation had given them authorization but not an obligation to provide such services. Section 79V of the Care Standards Act 2000 (the Act which transferred responsibility for regulation to Ofsted) required them to provide information to parents and support to providers either directly or by service agreements with others. These responsibilities were to be lodged in education departments. The new clarity on the responsibility to support the early years sector did much more than many had anticipated to galvanize local authorities into new action.

It was often in those local authorities where little had been offered in the way of support services before that the new early years teams were most dynamic and innovative. The role for education departments that was thus created was in many respects a more significant step in the switch of power and responsibility in the early years field to the education profession than the transfer of regulation to Ofsted.

The transfer to Ofsted took place after the general election in 2001. Of course, it took much longer for the advantages inherent in the new system to become reality. Nevertheless, it was in Blair's first term as prime minister that the change was planned and this decisive step can be seen in retrospect as one of the key events in the developing early years policy of his government.

2001–05: The second government of Tony Blair

For some people the changes introduced by the first Blair government were too tentative. To others it felt as though the government had steamed ahead with changes in an over-hasty manner. Those who devised the policies would probably draw from this the conclusion that they had got the pace of change about right. Once the election of 2001 had been won and the government had a new mandate, that pace quickened significantly.

Accelerating change was in part due to the development of arrangements that had been put in place before June 2001 when the election took place. Among these were the new arrangements for regulation, the work of early years teams in the education departments, the extension of the nursery grant scheme (so that quite quickly all children aged three or four had access to pre-school education), the development of local Sure Start projects and the work of the Qualifications and Curriculum Authority (QCA) in establishing both a proper framework for qualifications for early years practitioners (QCA, 1999) and the first stages of a Common Core Prospectus that could provide the unifying element for practitioners with a variety of specialisms within the early years field (QCA, 2004).

In addition there were measures taken to promote quality in provision. One of these was the publication of *Birth to Three Matters* (Sure Start Unit, 2002) and the accompanying work by DfES staff and others to encourage more careful consideration of the needs of the youngest children. This was an important and welcome step, giving official blessing to the views developed by researchers such as Goldschmied and Jackson (1994), Elfer (1997) and Elfer et al. (2003). There were also attempts, seen by many as inadequate, to bridge the gap between the Foundation Stage and Key Stage 1 (Evans, 2004a; 2004b; Featherstone, 2004; Tweed, 2003).

Outside central government there were moves among providers and their development support workers to improve practice in areas such as equal opportunities and a new emphasis on music and outdoor play, both of which had been widely under-valued before.

There were other developments that did not derive from government initiatives, but were more than compatible with its policy of partnership with the private sector. Probably the most significant of these was the growth of 'chains', that is, companies owning more than one setting, with a small number of companies achieving exponential growth, partly through building new units, but more often on the basis of taking over individual settings or smaller and more local chains. The chains were able to benefit from economies of scale in their professional development programmes, human resources work and premises design, and were better placed than small local nurseries to negotiate with central and local government agencies and thus make best use of schemes such as the Neighbourhood Nurseries Initiative.

These things, along with other measures – such as the efforts to recruit more men, disabled people and people from black and ethnic minorities into childcare – would have constituted a significant pattern of development in themselves. However, far more radical changes were introduced towards the end of the government's second term as it gained confidence.

Three documents were crucial in marking this shift in policy. One was the inter-departmental review of early years services in 2002 to which reference has already been made. This spoke of 'significant payoffs' from good quality early interventions for disadvantaged children and argued the need for new investment in childcare as well as claiming that structural reforms were needed in the system, among other reasons because of the weakness of EYDCPs and multi-agency work in general. The second was the report on the murder of Victoria Climbié (Laming, 2003). This might have become simply another report on a particularly shocking case of child abuse, highlighting some of the failures of official services (especially in the matter of cooperation between themselves) and urging everyone to do better. However, it came at a time that suited the government and was seized upon by them as yet more evidence of the need for an overarching policy on children and for radical institutional change. In picking up this highly publicized case, they probably also hoped to reassure those social workers who were worried that any new emphasis on family support and preventive measures would be at the expense of child protection. The third important document was the Green Paper issued after the Laming Report called *Every Child Matters* (DfES, 2003). All three documents were followed by the Children Act 2004 and before that by changes in the DfES and its work with local authorities and other agencies that did not necessarily require changes in the law.

The main elements in the policy that developed in the government's second term were institutional arrangements that embodied a focus on children as such in the delivery of services, an increased role for local authorities, an emphasis on coordination and the simplification of access to services and a new focus on parental responsibility.

Focusing on children

The government's early years policy in the first term had been founded to a significant extent on getting people off welfare and into work. This could be seen as placing the needs of children second, although the government was insistent that their objective of reducing child poverty did put children at the centre of concern. Many of the developments in the second term were based on the idea that more state structures should be arranged around children. This was new. In the 1960s and 1970s many official agencies had been reorganized around professions rather than categories of the population. A key example was the establishment in 1971 of the social services departments, which brought together a number of existing departments dealing with different client groups and was seen as marking the full emergence of social work as a profession. The focus of the changes now being introduced is on children and young people in general rather than children under eight. Nevertheless, there are considerable implications for the early years.

One of the first steps taken was to amalgamate Civil Service teams dealing with early years care and education into the new Sure Start Unit (Sure Start Unit, 2003). The name was criticized as causing confusion between the Sure Start projects and the overall programme for young children. The government responded that the projects had been pilots for the wider programme of early years services it was now introducing. They wanted to avoid the problems which led to the collapse of the Family Advice Centres and the Home Office Community Development Project in the 1970s by planning from the start to build on the pilot projects and make them the model for universal provision.

Other measures included the creation of a post of Minister for Children, the establishment of Children's Trusts in all local authority areas and the passing of the Children Act 2004 (which, among other things, laid the legislative basis for the post of a Children's Commissioner for England), the creation of Children's Services Authorities in all local authorities, the establishment of new statutory Local Safeguarding Children Boards replacing the ACPCs and developing a new integrated framework for the inspection of all services for children.

There were also changes in service delivery. In 2003 the government announced its intention of establishing a Children's Centre in every local authority ward, starting with the 20 per cent of wards across the country that were considered to be most deprived on the basis of statistical criteria. The rest would follow later. The centres were not necessarily buildings, as their purpose was to provide better coordination and development rather than new premises. Nevertheless, plans for the first batch of centres nearly all entailed focus on particular premises, usually those that were already designated Early Excellence Centres, Neighbourhood Nurseries Initiative units or the bases for local Sure Start projects.

A new role for local authorities

From what has been said already it will be apparent that the government had decided to give a more central role to local authorities (initially in the education departments, by the end of 2005 in the Children's Services departments) in the development of early years services. This represented a change of mind brought about partly by disillusion with the EYDCPs, and partly by a positive appreciation of the work done by the best early years teams in the education departments.

However, there were limitations to this. Local authorities were to share their leading role with others, especially with community health services. Their primary functions were to be in planning, coordination and support, and not (except in the case of extended schools) in direct provision. There was less detailed guidance from the DfES on how local plans should be developed than there had been, but it remained clear that the direction would be set by Whitehall.

Coordination and simplification of access to services

The experience of the EYDCPs may have been seen by government as problematic, but it remained committed to the principle of partnership. Many of the initiatives taken after 2003 were designed to force upon early years practitioners, and even more on the wider professions of education, social work and community health, the need to cooperate more fully than they had done previously. The government was beginning to feel more confident that it could push people into collaborative planning, that it could insist (in the vision that underpinned the idea of Children's Centres in particular) on coordination to secure simplicity of access to parents, and even that it could begin to edge nearer to the idea of a single early years profession embracing day-care staff, teachers and perhaps even playworkers as discussed further in Chapter 5. This work in relation to children has to be seen in a wider context. The government was promoting similar initiatives in other areas of concern. Under the Local Government Act (2000), local authorities in England had been given new powers to promote well-being in their areas, to establish new structures that would facilitate coordination between council services and to subscribe to new codes of conduct. The government sought to build on this legislative base in its second term. A key step was the establishment of a number of Local Area Agreements (the first 20 being finalized just before the general election of 2005) which represented an attempt to secure genuine debate and cooperation between central government and local authorities on objectives for the areas they served. Local authorities began to devise overall strategies in cooperation with other local organizations and interests. Some of this was done through exercises in public consultation or informal discussion. The standard pattern was for local partnership boards to be created. These usually had more specialist partnership boards attached to them, including boards dealing with children and young people. Towards the end of the second Blair government coordination between those working for and with young children and their families was increasingly taking place in the context of this overall pattern of discussion and coordination.

Focus on parents

There was also a strengthened focus on parents. In 1989 the Children Act had substituted the legal concept of 'parental responsibility' for that of 'parental rights'. This broad change was fully in line with the views of the Labour government, which differed from that of the previous Conservative governments only in insisting that many parents needed more assistance to meet their responsibilities. However, there was also a greater readiness to take punitive steps against parents of older children who behaved in an anti-social manner or truanted from school. At the same time support was given to positive parenting by the local Sure Start projects and by other initiatives, such as the Basic Skills Agency's Early Start project (Brooks et al., 2004).

One indication of the shift in thinking lay in statements by ministers on the matter of working mothers. When Margaret Thatcher was prime minister, statements by members of her government often suggested that any single mothers who went out to work were failing their children. In the first term that Tony Blair was prime minister the contrary was often suggested – that single mothers who did not seek opportunities to work were failing their children by condemning them to life on benefits. After the election of 2001 more positive statements were made about mothers who chose to stay at home and steps were proposed about the basis of pension calculations and about parental (rather than just maternity) leave that were designed to give mothers more freedom of choice on the matter of how soon they should return to work after their children were born. However, the basic thrust of policy was to encourage single parents back to paid employment.

The changing scope of early years policy

The focus on the role of parents and the pressure to secure greater collaboration between health service and local authority professions in this sphere represented a significant shift in the way in which early years services were conceived. For most of the recent past they had meant day care for children under eight, education for pre-school children (and, perhaps, at Key Stage 1) and some aspects of playwork. The scope of 'early years' is now changing and must be taken to include a variety of forms of direct support to parents; especially those offered by health visitors and other health service personnel.

The Labour Party in power after 2005

Tony Blair won a third general election victory in 2005, but – for better or for worse – never had the opportunity to pursue the development of a programme of reform in the public services he had intended. Had he done so, the impact on early years services might have been considerable. As it was, his final years in power were overshadowed by the political fall-out from the war in Iraq, which was going badly, and unavoidable debate as to when he would go and which of his ministers would replace him. He finally stepped down in 2007 and was replaced by Gordon Brown.

From the election victory in 2005 to the time that work was undertaken on this second edition (in the first half of 2008) there were two major initiatives impacting on early years work.

One was the production of new guidance on the curriculum for the Foundation Stage, which came into operation in September 2008. The new document:

▸ Dealt with the curriculum for children from birth to five. It was thus based on a combination of two existing documents, *Birth to Three Matters* and the older curriculum guidance for children aged three and four.

▸ Represented some kind of compromise in the continuing battle between those who wanted to defer what was usually called 'formal' education until the sixth or even seventh year and those who wanted children to acquire basic skills as early as possible. Being a compromise it failed to please entirely either side. Influential figures in the early years world denounced it as 'too prescriptive'. David Cameron, the new leader of the Conservative Party, called for efforts to achieve literacy at a very early age and for the achievement of literacy itself to be based on synthetic phonics.

▸ Made a slight dent in the distinction between school and pre-school, by making it the guidance that should govern the teaching of children up until the September after their fifth birthday, thus creating a situation where a child close to his/her sixth birthday should still be governed by this guidance rather than the National Curriculum.

▸ Made changes in the system of regulation that further eroded the artificial distinction between care and education.

▸ Had a much longer lead-in period than similar documents in the recent past in an effort to avoid unnecessary confusion when it became operational.

The other major initiative was the division (after Gordon Brown became prime minister) of the old DfES into two separate ministries – one dealing with children, schools and families, the other with further and higher education. This step underlined the fact that the government had intended the move to create children's services departments at local level to be a significant one. The new ministry was in all respects a body intended to be parallel to the new local authority departments. Its very existence formed a message to interested parties that the new children's services departments were not to be the old education departments with a few more bits added on, even if the cost of providing schools would inevitably remain by far the highest element in the budgets of the new departments. Gordon Brown marked the significance of the new ministry by giving it to Ed Balls, one of his closest political allies. Balls, in his turn, underlined the message by issuing a number of policy statements on issues other than schooling in his first few weeks in office.

Apart from these two major changes, the principal developments in policy in the period after the general election of 2005 involved the consolidation and full implementation of the changes introduced during the second Blair government. This included:

▸ the work of the new children's services departments

▸ the continued roll-out of local children's centres and of the overall Sure Start programme

▸ further work on the qualifications framework and the development of a new single early years profession

▶ the consolidation of the new systems for safeguarding children

▶ improved cooperation between different agencies by means of Local Area Agreements, local Partnership Boards and locally devised strategies

▶ the work of the Children's Commissioners in the different parts of the UK.

The developments that have occurred have given rise to controversy in the professional press and occasionally in the wider media. There are other policy issues that have scarcely found their way onto the agenda. These include the political dimension of quality issues which are seen all too often as a matter of merely technical concern (Dahlberg et al., 1999); the question of whether the voluntary and community sector can hold its own against big business; and the question of whether parents can develop a voice as citizens saying how services should develop in the interests of everyone or whether they will remain merely consumers of the services provided.

The criticisms that are made of current policy, mainly by lobbyists, the issues that have not yet fully surfaced and the continued tendency of sections of the media to emphasize negative news stories about childcare demonstrate that policy in the early years field remains controversial. However, in many ways the pattern that has been set since 1997 seems likely to remain in place for some time with a widespread consensus in favour of:

▶ universal provision of day care and education for young children

▶ an established lead role for the education profession

▶ direct provision by both local authorities and the independent sector

▶ much greater coordination in the planning and delivery of services

▶ more services to assist parents directly in meeting their responsibilities.

The statements made by all three major political parties during the general election campaign of 2005 about their policies on children were striking not because of the differences between them, but because all three agreed that early years services were among the most important for which any new government would be responsible. There were differences and others have emerged since, with new leaders taking over each of the three major political parties. However, such differences pale into insignificance in comparison with the broader consensus that now exists and which it would have been difficult to envisage even towards the end of the 1990s.

Summary ☐

This chapter has shown how:

▶ the nature as well as the scale of early years services have changed dras-
tically over the period of modern history

▶ the pace of change escalated over the last ten years of the twentieth century and the first few years of the twenty-first century

▶ while controversies remain, there is now a significant degree of consensus among the major political parties on the importance of those services
and, to some extent, the ways in which they should be encouraged and
organized.

The next chapter deals with the social and political forces that lie behind that
process of change.

Further reading

As was said at the beginning of this chapter, there is no general history of the
development of early years services in this country and this makes it difficult
to recommend further reading. However, the following titles are useful:

Heywood, C. (2001) *A History of Childhood: Children and Childhood in the West
from Medieval to Modern Times*, Cambridge: Polity Press in association with
Oxford: Blackwell Publishing. A good introduction to the general background.

Cunningham, H. (2006) *The Invention of Childhood*, London: BBC Books. The
book is based on series broadcast on Radio 4 and a CD version of those
broadcasts is also available.

David, T. (ed.) (1994) *Working Together for Young Children: Multi-professionalism in Action*, London: Routledge. A collection of essays offering a good
picture of the situation a few years before the general election of 1997 and
which can be used as a source book for those who want to understand the
extent of change over the decade that followed its publication.

Jones, M. and Lowe, R. (2002) *From Beveridge to Blair: The First Fifty Years of
Britain's Welfare State 1948–98*, Manchester: Manchester University Press.
Offers useful background on the general development of social policy up to
the period soon after Tony Blair's first election victory, although it has little
on the period since 1997 and, like most books on social policy published so
far, has little to say on early years services.

Key dates in the development of early years policy

1945
- Labour government supplants wartime coalition
- Ministry of Health Circular 221/45 speaks of positively discouraging mothers of children under two from working
- Responsibility for running day nurseries transfers from central to local government, but with 50% cut in funding

1946
- National Health Service Act as part of new NHS empowers local authorities to set up day care for young children in need

1948
- Nurseries and Child-Minders Regulation Act sets up system of regulation for first time under the public health departments
- Children Act sets up local authority children's departments (absorbed into social services departments (SSDs) in 1971)

1951
- Conservative general election victory

1962
- Pre-school Playgroups Association (now Pre-School Learning Alliance) formed

1963
- Children and Young Persons Act (among other things) lays legislative basis for Family Advice Centres

1964
- Labour Party wins general election

1965
- Child Poverty Action Group founded

1967
- *0–5: Report on the Care of Pre-School Children* (Yudkin Report) on risks of accidental harm to children in day care
- Plowden Report on primary education issues

1968
- Health Services and Public Health Act tightens regulation of day care and minders for young children

1970
- Conservative Party wins general election

continued

continued

1971   • SSDs start operation

1972   • White Paper *Education: A Framework for Expansion* urges education departments to cooperate more closely with voluntary and community sector

1973   • Keith Joseph's first 'Cycle of Deprivation' speech

1974   • Labour Party wins general election
        • SSDs assume full responsibility for regulation of pre-school day care and childminding

1976   • DES/DHSS Report *Low Cost Day provision for the Under Fives*
        • National Conference at Sunningdale speaks of dangers of emotional deprivation for children in day care, and is highly influential on policy for many years afterwards

1977   • DES/DHSS report on 'Combined Nursery Schools and Day Centres'
        • National Childminding Association formed

1978   • Government Circular on coordination of services for children

1979   • Conservatives win general election and those that follow to stay in power until 1997
        • Failed attempts to introduce devolution in Scotland and Wales

1980   • National Daycare Trust Formed

1981   • Education Act (among other things) gives local authorities a duty to provide for children under five with learning difficulties

1985   • Kids' Club Network (now 4Children) formed

1986   • 'Integrated' young children's service established in Strathclyde

continued

continued

1987 • *Children Under Five: Educational Research and Evidence* (Clark Report) speaks of need for greater coordination of services

1988 • National Curriculum introduced in schools

1989 • Children Act 1989 (among other things) extends system of regulation of early years day care and childminding
• Adoption of the UN Convention on the Rights of the Child

1990 • Rumbold Report Published
• Scottish Childminding Association formed

1991 • Volume 2 (on regulation of day care and childminding) of the Guidance and Regulations for the Children Act published by Department of Health
• Number of playgroups and childminders peaks nationally

1992 • Schools Act (establishes Ofsted)

1993 • LAC 1993/1: Government Circular accusing local authorities of being too rigid in regulation of day care and childminding
• *First Class* (Report on reception classes by Ofsted) speaks of importance of play

1994 • Code of Practice on Children with Special Educational Needs published

1995 • Hearing in the High Court confirms that the official Guidance and Regulations on registration and inspection do not have force of law

1996 • *Desirable outcomes for children's learning on entering compulsory education* (Schools Curriculum and Assessment Authority)
• Nursery Education and Grant-Maintained Schools Act establishes voucher system for nursery education

1997 • Labour Party wins general election
• Initial guidance issued on what were to become Early Years Development and Childcare Partnerships

continued

continued

1998
- Launch of Quality Projects strategy
- National Childcare Strategy published
- Consultation Paper on future of system of regulation of early years services published
- National Literacy Strategy introduced
- Responsibility for early years passes from Department of Health to Department for Education and Skills
- Legislation for devolution in Scotland and Wales

1999
- Working Families Tax Credit introduced
- National Early Years Training Organization established
- Protection of Children Act passed
- National Numeracy Strategy introduced
- Work on 'qualifications framework' for early years begins
- Government announces that responsibility for regulation of early years services will pass to Ofsted
- National Day Nurseries Association launched

2000
- Start-up grants for childminders announced
- *Curriculum Guidance for the Foundation Stage* published
- Care Standards Act (among other things) lays legislative basis for transfer of responsibility for regulation to Ofsted (in England) and the Welsh Assembly (in Wales)
- First draft of new National Standards for Day Care and Childminding Published

2001
- Responsibility for regulation of day care and childminding passed to Ofsted
- Local authorities obliged for the first time to provide information, advice and training services in early years field
- First Children's Commissioner for Wales appointed
- Publication by Scottish Executive of policy document *For Scotland's Children*

2002
- Criminal Records Bureau begins work
- Education Act allows schools to provide day care
- *Birth to Three Matters* published
- Guidance on Children's Trusts issued
- Government Inter-Departmental Review of Childcare Published
- Unified Sure Start Unit established in DfES

continued

continued

2003	• Laming Report on Victoria Climbié case
	• Green Paper *Every Child Matters* published
	• Announcement of 'Children's Centres' programme
	• Children's Commissioner for Northern Ireland takes up post

2003
- Laming Report on Victoria Climbié case
- Green Paper *Every Child Matters* published
- Announcement of 'Children's Centres' programme
- Children's Commissioner for Northern Ireland takes up post

2004
- 'Common Core Prospectus' for early years drafted
- Bichard Report on the Soham murders published
- System for 'light touch' regulation of nannies announced
- EPPE (Effective Provision of Pre-School Education) Report published
- Government's Ten-year Strategy for Childcare published
- Children Act 2004
- Children's Commissioner for Scotland appointed
- Childcare Working Group set up by Assembly Government in Wales

2005
- Children's Commissioner for England appointed
- Announcement of changes to the periods between inspection of care and education services for young children
- England's Children's Commissioner starts work
- General election – Labour Party wins third term in office
- Children's Workforce Development Council for England starts work
- National Sure Start evaluation published

2006
- Outline framework of new EYFS published
- 2006 Childcare Act
- First cohorts of candidates finish secure EYPS
- Welsh Assembly publishes strategic plan for education 2006–2010
- Renewed Framework for Literacy and Mathematics

2007
- Critical report on children's centres by National Audit Office
- UNICEF report ranks UK bottom out of 21 wealthy nation in terms of well-being of children
- Ofsted becomes the new Office for Standards in Education, Children's Services and Skills
- New SNP Government in Scotland appoints country's first Minister for Children and Early Years
- New prime minister Gordon Brown splits DfES. First Secretary of State for Children, Schools and Families appointed
- Final Version of Welsh Foundation Stage published
- New qualifications framework for Scotland published
- Department for Education in Northern Ireland assumes responsibility for Sure Start in the province

2008
- Implementation of new EYFS in England

Figure 2.1 *Key dates in the development of early years policy*

Chapter 3

Influences on Early Years Policy Development

This chapter explores:

▶ the range of influences on the formation and development of early years policy

▶ the ways in which policy is developed

▶ the first two levels of policy-making as described in Chapter 1 (underlying factors and broad objectives). The third level (detailed arrangements required to meet those objectives) is discussed in Chapter 4.

In this chapter we explore case studies of policy development to demonstrate who is involved in policy-making and how particular policies come into being. The social and cultural contexts of early years policy development are discussed along with the influence of social change and public opinion on the policy process. The roles of central and local government and key government agencies are also discussed with reference to the influence of early years agencies, organizations, practitioners and academics on how policy is developed.

The development of early years policy is often part of much wider policy agendas, and the goals of early years policy may be broader than simply developing and structuring services for young children and their families. For example, within the current political agenda, much of the recent development of early years services has been part of a much bigger strategy to tackle poverty and raise standards of educational outcomes for children. Often the aims of policy are multi-layered and complex, interweaving early years developments with other linked social goals.

Since 1997, the development of early years services has been part of a policy agenda, the aims of which include:

▶ improving educational standards, particularly basic skills, especially among socially disadvantaged children

▶ increasing employability among school-leavers and reducing the number of NEETS (not in employment, education or training) aged 16–24

- ▶ providing childcare so parents (particularly mothers) can go to work, education or training

- ▶ reducing the number of people dependent on the state in both the short and the long term

- ▶ ensuring better standards of health and welfare for all children

- ▶ reducing anti-social behaviour and crime rates.

Recent developments in early years policy cannot be viewed in isolation from this wider agenda to tackle social exclusion. But, why is it important to have an understanding of where early years policy comes from, and what determines the content of such policy? Practitioners need to understand the varied and interrelated factors influencing policy development in the early years in order to be able to understand their own and others' roles in this process. It is also important to recognize that policy is neither exempt from trends nor made in isolation but that it is a product of the prevailing social context within which it develops. Practitioners need to understand that policy will change and develop; that it can be questioned; can be considered wrong; and can be influenced by their own views and actions.

Early years policy as a social construct

Social policies, including early years policies, are not created in a vacuum but develop within a historical, cultural and ideological framework. Policy is subject to trends and the influence of dominant viewpoints. It is based on previous policy, which may continue to shape it. It may be influenced by single events or long-term trends. It can be influenced by feedback from those who implement it or research by academics or practitioners. Policy is not developed outside 'real life' but is dependent on what happens in practice while at the same time influencing this.

Early years policy can be described as a social construct because its nature and content are dependent at any point in time on the social and cultural context within which it is made and implemented. As such, early years policy will change over time and develop within the society in which it is made. Early years policy is subject not only to wider social and cultural trends and developments, but also specific events within the field of early years. Often policy developments are the result of the interactions between a complex range of factors.

Historical perspectives on early years policy, like any other policy, are dependent on viewing past events from the ideology and value-systems of the present, resulting in changed perceptions of the relevance of those policies. For example,

Moss (2003) discusses how childcare policy has changed over time and how 'best practice' in the past seems 'grotesquely inappropriate' today. Moss concludes:

> care – policy and practice is situated within particular temporal, spatial and cultural contexts. What we see as best practice today may not seem so in another generation, nor will it necessarily be viewed as such from the perspectives of those countries and groups who prefer different approaches or who have different traditions. An historical perspective is a reminder of the provisional and contingent status of all policies, and the practices and provisions to which they give rise. (Moss, 2003: 16)

For example, one of the authors remembers visiting a residential nursery in the 1970s where children under two were cared for either because they were waiting to be placed for adoption or because they were in the short- or long-term care of the local authority. At the time, this type of care was diminishing rapidly as changing views of the needs of infants, particularly around attachment needs, led to the development of policies which determined that all young children should be placed in family care. Within current thinking, this type of group care of young infants goes against everything we know about the needs of children of this age, exemplified by the human rights outcry against such nurseries in countries like Romania and China. However, in the past, young children were routinely raised in orphanages and children's homes, sometimes from birth, and this was considered a positive aspect of child welfare.

In the next section, the various influences on early years policy development are illustrated in an extended case study of how Sure Start Local Programmes were developed. This case study is intended to demonstrate the ways in which a range of influences shape policy development at a particular time and how these influences interact with each other.

Case study of early years policy development: Sure Start Local Programmes

One early years policy development that clearly exemplifies the varied range of interrelated factors which come together to influence policy at a particular point in time and place is that of Sure Start Local Programmes (SSLPs). This highly significant development in early years policy evolved in the way it did because of the conjunction of a range of events at a time when the political agenda created an opportunity for this type of project. In 1997, the New Labour government came to power with a remit to tackle poverty and social exclusion. They instituted a comprehensive spending review to look at how public money was being spent and to make reforms to take into account the spending priorities of the new government. Although most of this review was on a department-by-department

continued

continued

basis, some areas of policy, such as early years, were not the responsibility of one department and so were subject to 'cross-cutting' reviews across a number of departments. The early years 'cross-cutting' review was also influenced by the perception that early years services were failing the most needy children and families. The departments involved were many:

> As well as the obvious departments like health (including personal social services), education and employment (including childcare), there were also social security (benefits for children and families), environment, transport and the regions (urban regeneration and housing), home office (policy on the family), the Lord Chancellor's Department (family law), culture, media and sport (children's play) and the Treasury (the money) – not forgetting the Scots, Welsh and Northern Irish, each with their own subtly different mix of policies. (Glass, 1999: 2)

The sheer number of departments involved led to the appointment of Tessa Jowell, the Minister for Public Health, as the chair of the group, not as departmental representative, but in her own right. This was significant in that she strongly influenced changes in the remit to look at under sevens and refocused the review on birth to threes and pre-conception as the period most likely to influence long-term changes in outcomes for children. Although usually this type of review would mainly have been done through relevant departments as outlined above, early in the review many other agencies became involved either through being contacted by government officials or through their own interventions. This meant that the development of SSLPs was influenced right from the start by organizations such as the Pre-School Learning Alliance (PLA), National Children's Bureau (NCB), various early years services, and academics involved in the field. This involvement by those in practice led to a series of seminars where government officials and ministers met with those directly involved in early years services from 'a wide range of disciplines including child development, social work, health and demography as well as practitioners and local politicians' (Glass, 1999: 3). It also led to the commissioning of a review of research into 'what worked' to support children and families by Marjorie Smith of the Thomas Coram Research Unit (Smith et al., 1998).

The result of all this range of activity was the conclusion, in the review, that services needed to be developed to support children and families in their earliest years of life to combat multiple disadvantages that had a significant negative influence on children's life chances. Such services needed to be consistently targeted on under fours where service provision had been persistently neglected and which was, as a result, fragmented and unevenly

continued

continued

distributed geographically. Other factors found to be significant in the delivery of such services were the need to provide community-based services, to involve parents and provide family support at a high level. Developments also needed to be long term, sustainable, multi-disciplinary and culturally sensitive.

The influence of the US Head Start programme, which had been running since 1965, was also highly significant in the development of Sure Start. The Head Start programmes had been developed to support pre-school children from low-income families to improve educational attainments and general health and welfare. Early Head Start had been established in 1995 to extend the pro-gramme to children aged from birth to three and pregnant women. The development of SSLPs drew much from the structure and philosophy of Head Start, particularly the child-focused and multi-agency approach.

And so the SSLPs were born and with them the start of the government's later wide-ranging Sure Start initiative. Some of the key factors influencing policy development which resulted in the establishment of SSLPs, were:

- a newly elected government with a mandate to tackle social exclusion
- the decision to look at young children's needs across departments (the cross-cutting review)
- the review of research on 'what works' for young children
- the extensive involvement of agencies and practitioners in that review.

The commitment to SSLPs has been significant, reflected in the growth of the number of programmes. Between the initial 250 established in 1999 and the sixth 'wave' in 2003 a total of 524 SSLPs were set up in the 20 per cent most disadvantaged wards in the country.

Evaluation of the SSLPs has been achieved through a six-year long project, the National Evaluation of Sure Start (NESS). Earlier reports showed that there were mixed results with inconsistencies between SSLPs and some evidence that SSLPs may have failed to reach the most disadvantaged families they sought to support. Evidence showed positive developments in terms of involv-ing parents but a more mixed and less successful set of outcomes for partnership between agencies. More recently the NESS team reported that SSLPs had been successful in that:

- Parents of three-year-old children showed less negative parenting while providing their children with a better home learning environment.
- Three-year-old children in SSLP areas had better social development with higher levels of positive social behaviour and independence/self-regulation than children in similar areas not having an SSLP.

continued

continued

▸ The SSLP effects for positive social behaviour appeared to be a consequence of the SSLP benefits upon parenting.

▸ Three-year-old children in SSLP areas had higher immunisation rates and fewer accidental injuries than children in similar areas not having an SSLP.

▸ Families living in SSLP areas used more child- and family-related services than those living elsewhere (adapted from NESS Research Team, 2008: 1).

Sure Start Children's Centres

After 2003, existing SSLPs and other existing provision such as neighbourhood nurseries and Early Excellence Centres have been transforming into Sure Start Children's Centres, in response to further policy developments which seek to mainstream the types of provision developed through SSLPs. In 2002, the Sure Start Unit and Early Years and Childcare Unit had merged to integrate Sure Start and government childcare strategies.

Children's Centres are rolling out across the country, with over 2,900 established in the most disadvantaged areas already and one in every community (3,500) planned for 2010. The development of Children's Centres has been placed firmly within local authorities, in that since 2004 they have been responsible for 'co-ordinating local planning and carrying accountability for delivery' (Arnold, 2005: 7). In addition, developing leadership in children's centres has been a key focus for ensuring effective change management with the establishment of the National Professional Qualification in Integrated Centre Management (NPQICL) through the National College for School Leadership piloted in 2004 and rolled out to Children's Centre managers from 2005 onwards.

The development of Children's Centres is based on establishing holistic services for families and children under five, aiming to provide:

▸ affordable, quality childcare and education

▸ health and family support services

▸ services for children and families with special needs

▸ co-located, integrated service provision to better meet the needs of all children and families and to provide early assessment and intervention for children with additional needs.

This can be seen as a particular example of the application of the principles associated with *Every Child Matters* that it should be possible for all children to be healthy, safe, enjoying achievement, making a positive contribution and achieving economic well-being. The aim in this case is to develop integrated mainstream services for all children, which will also better support the children and families most in need. In order to promote this, development work was done on mainstreaming Sure Start principles and practice through seven pilots running between 2002 and 2004. While the actual services provided varied, the pilots all focused on:

▸ developing parenting and family support

▸ training paraprofessionals (front-line workers such as early years practitioners) to provide services such as speech therapy

▸ co-locating and integrating service provision (including health)

▸ developing databases

▸ multi-disciplinary training (Sure Start, 2008).

The evaluation of the mainstreaming pilots provided feedback relevant for the development of Children's Centres:

▸ using existing local strategic networks was more effective than trying to build new ones

▸ the need for cross-agency steering groups, pilot co-ordinators and project managers to keep new developments on track

▸ feedback systems to monitor progress

▸ early planning and development of mainstreaming strategies

▸ time and resources for frontline staff

▸ regard for both national and local policy and priorities

▸ champions for mainstreaming Sure Start approaches and making the case for change (White et al., 2005).

One of the key arguments for moving from SSLPs focused on disadvantaged areas to universal Children's Centres is that some children and families with needs who lived outside Sure Start areas did not get a service. However, the development of Children's Centres led to a number of concerns about the loss of SSLPs as they stood. These concerns focused on several areas:

▸ Spending is now much lower per child as budgets are more thinly spread.

▸ Parental involvement and the role of the voluntary and community sectors were seen as under threat under local authority control.

▶ Services would be less focused on the most needy and would be more focused on childcare and parental employability.

▶ Prescriptive guidelines would lead to fewer local choices.

▶ Professionals from some other agencies, particularly health, were not employed by the Children's Centres and therefore it may be more difficult to secure effective services.

An evaluation of Children's Centres by the National Audit Office (NAO), published in 2006, found:

▶ most families were happy with the quality of services and centres were meeting the needs of some families

▶ fathers, ethnic minority groups (in areas where they were a smaller part of the population), families of children with disabilities and families with the highest level of needs were not yet having their needs met across the centres

▶ not all centres had developed effective working arrangements with health and employment services

▶ leadership challenges in developing effective inter-professional cooperation needed to be met

▶ difficulties in measuring cost-effectiveness of services.

Similarly, Ofsted (2006a) found that Children's Centres were meeting children's needs and were generally well managed, but that measuring the outcomes of extended services posed a challenge as did short-term funding. They found that 'The most successful providers shaped the provision gradually to reflect their community's needs and wants in collaboration with other agencies' (Ofsted, 2006a: 3).

In early 2008, Ofsted reported again on the progress of Children's Centres, finding that:

▶ centres were generally successful in promoting the five *Every Child Matters* outcomes

▶ parents were positive about the childcare on offer and children using the centres were generally well-prepared for school.

However, although local authorities supported setting up of centres, Ofsted (2008) found that they gave less support for monitoring and evaluation, and despite performance management guidance issued in late 2006 this continued to be an area for development for centres (DfES, 2006). The guidance aims to support clearer monitoring and evaluation to ensure that services also reach the most disadvantaged groups and that outcomes for children's achievement can be tracked.

The Office for Standards in Education also found that:

- ▶ services within centres are not always well coordinated and this may be affecting take-up

- ▶ not all types of families are using the centres fully, with ethnic minority groups and families with disabilities less likely to.

Despite these ongoing issues, Children's Centres are generally proving to provide for the holistic needs of many young children and their families and continue to be supported at national level as a key factor in implementing the *Every Child Matters: Change for Children* (DfES, 2004b) agenda.

Factors influencing early years policy development

As exemplified in the case study above, SSLPs were established through the conjunction of a range of influences at a particular place and point in time. In the case study, one of the key factors was the complex interaction between political agendas, politicians, civil servants and the professional groups who became involved in the process of developing SSLPs. The election of the New Labour government in 1997 had resulted in a shift of political objectives and placed individuals with an interest in developing services for young children in positions of power. This provided a forum for the views of professional organizations such as the NCB and the Thomas Coram Foundation to become more influential.

Factors influencing policy development do not operate independently, but form systems, which create policy unique to themselves. A system can be defined as a set of elements interacting to achieve a goal. The components of a system are the elements that are involved in the processes of the system, which can affect the system and may be affected by it (Levine and Fitzgerald, 1992). For example, in the development of SSLPs the elements involved in this process included the work of the cross-cutting review and the contributions of politicians, civil servants, practitioners, agencies and researchers (Figure 3.1). However, within systems theory there is a belief that in order to understand some events we need not just to see the elements contributing to an event but also to see the whole, recognizing patterns and interrelationships between the elements (Senge and Lannon-Kim, 1991). In the case study, the important feature of the policy development was not just who or which agencies were involved in the process, but the nature and quality of the interrelationships between these. A key feature of this development was the communication that took place between different elements and the ways in which beliefs about how the needs of children and families could be best met were shaped by these communications. The development of SSLPs was not just based on ideas about how children's needs could be best met but also on perceived failures of previous policy.

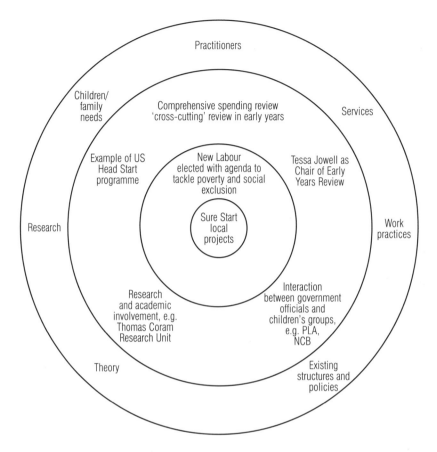

Figure 3.1 *Systems diagram of development of Sure Start*

As was said at the end of Chapter 2, it is important to remember that, nationally, governments determine the direction of early years policy and the ways in which other influences come to bear on government plans are complex. It is clear that the influence of factors such as lobbying by professional organizations and academic research may have no significant impact on policy development until they coincide with political agendas. The ways in which political agendas are shaped and developed are discussed below.

The social and cultural context of early years policy

One of the most significant influences on early years policy is the social and cultural context in which policy is made. Social and cultural changes over time shape views and attitudes towards how children and families should behave and be supported. One of the driving forces behind more recent policy in the early years has been changes in how childcare is seen in terms of its value to children and families and changes in attitudes towards working mothers.

Moss (2003) identifies three social norms which have influenced the development of childcare policy over time:

▸ Individualized care of children within the family.

▸ Gender division of labour.

▸ National economic survival.

The changing nature of the relationship between these norms has been significant in shaping early years policy development. In the UK, the strong cultural belief in family responsibility for children and the privacy of the family as an institution has been punctuated by the state's assumption of responsibility for children where families are seen to have failed in their duty of care. Until 1997, this meant that care of children outside the home had for a long time been seen as a last resort for children; undesirable but necessary in some cases (Daycare Trust, 2005). However, attitudes towards childcare have more recently been reconfigured towards the view that such care is a positive contribution to all children's welfare, rather than a compensation for poor standards of parenting. This sea change in attitudes towards childcare has come about partly through the necessity of bringing women into a labour force hungry for new recruits in order to meet Moss's third norm, national economic survival. Acceptance of childcare as a universal benefit to children was aided by the integration of early years education and care and the growing belief that early learning is crucial to positive educational outcomes for children later on.

However, the belief that maternal care was best dominated early years policy for many decades. The concept of the superiority of one-to-one care of children within the family has largely hinged on perceptions of women's gender roles within the family and workforce. Historically, early years policy has been strongly influenced by views on the role of women and the 'best' care of young children. The belief that young children should be cared for by their mothers until school age has been highly significant in the development of childcare policy throughout the period between the Second World War and the 1980s (Moss, 2003). For example, most of the day nurseries that opened during the Second World War to allow women to work while men fought closed rapidly after the war finished as women were encouraged to return to their traditional roles, which included caring for children.

Even the Plowden Report (DES, 1967), which led to the expansion of nursery education through an increase in places, clearly stated that part-time places should be offered because they discouraged women from working, and children needed to be with their mothers at least part of the day. Only in an exceptional and limited number of cases where financial need overruled the objections to mother–child separation were full-time places considered. Although the report recognized the strong links between social class and educational success, it also emphasized the role of nurseries in compensating for disadvantage rather than as a universal service for all young children. The Plowden Report continued to influence nursery education until the 1990s by perpetuating the split between education and care; ignoring the under-threes; and ignoring the needs of working parents.

The principle that children were best off at home with their mothers was challenged by the steady rise in numbers of women working from the 1970s onwards as, increasingly, women's wages became an essential part of the family income. In addition to individual families needing to increase their incomes, changing roles of women driven by the women's movement throughout the 1970s and 1980s, and changing labour market needs have resulted in social changes around perceptions of women's gender roles. More recently, the need to fill gaps in the labour market with increased numbers of women workers has been a strong factor in policy development. Demographic changes have led to concerns relating to national survival in terms of meeting labour market needs and supporting the increasing proportion of older people in the UK. As Brannen and Moss (2003) point out, an increased focus on early years policy has been partly influenced by falling birth rates and an ageing population.

Although women continue to have the main responsibility for young children, large numbers are in the workforce. In the UK, 68 per cent of women with dependent children are in the workforce compared with 76 per cent of those without (Office for National Statistics, 2003). Women are more likely than men to work part-time, particularly if they have dependent children. Nearly 40 per cent of women with dependent children work part-time compared with 23 per cent of those without.

Women's changing role in the labour market has influenced the development of early years services as demand for childcare rose steadily through the 1980s onwards. In the absence of a coherent policy to support the growing need for childcare the growth of private day nurseries filled some of this gap, but this has only met the needs of better-off families with well-paid jobs, as the costs of private day care have not been affordable for many parents. The introduction of tax benefits to reduce childcare costs to parents has improved this situation for some parents but the cost of childcare remains outside the reach of many families (Daycare Trust, 2005).

The availability and affordability of childcare places for less well-off families continues to be a thorny problem for many, despite the growth of places since the National Childcare Strategy and other subsequent childcare policies. Traditionally, families have relied on relatives to help out with childcare but there are fewer extended families and higher levels of geographical mobility now. As a result, fewer parents can rely on relatives to help out with childcare and their reliance on other forms of care has increased.

Other social trends have significance for the development of early years policy. Pugh (2001) identifies increasing numbers of children on or below the poverty line in the last 25 years as one of four key issues influencing how children are growing up at the beginning of the twenty-first century. So why is child poverty such a significant issue at this point in time?

Child poverty grew in the UK between the late 1970s and through to the 1990s in response to market-driven economic strategies and low investment in education, health and welfare for children. This growth in child poverty was widespread, with one in three children living in poverty in 1998 as compared to one in ten in 1979. However, since 1999, when Blair announced his intention to eradicate child poverty, 600,000 children have been lifted out of poverty. Despite this significant improvement, 28 per cent of children in Britain still live in poverty (3.5 million children) making this one of the worst rates in the industrialized world (End Child Poverty, 2005). As such, eradication of child poverty remains one of the driving forces behind government policy at the current time.

One of the key elements of poverty reduction is the raft of 'welfare to work' policies designed to support parents in gaining employment. Poverty was once most associated with lack of work in families, but now 52 per cent of children living in poverty are in households with one adult working. To avoid poverty, families need to have more than one adult working and/or in well-paid employment. The number of workers in low-paid jobs has doubled since 1977 with over 6 million people on low wages (one-fifth of the workforce) (End Child Poverty, 2005). Poverty is strongly linked to an inability to access well-paid work, with the gap between 'work rich' and 'work poor' families growing steadily. As part of the 'welfare to work' policy programme, early years services have been expanded to facilitate the return to work of more parents, particularly mothers.

Poverty has an impact on many aspects of children's lives, including health and educational outcomes. It plays a key role in social exclusion and the 'cycle of deprivation' through which social exclusion impacts on children's lives from one generation to the next. The price of high levels of poverty is seen in high unemployment figures, high benefits bills, a poorly skilled workforce and family breakdown. High levels of poverty are linked to high crime figures and anti-social behaviour among children and young people.

The outcomes of poverty are significant for children, with one-third of all children:

▸ not having three meals a day

▸ missing out on toys, activities and school trips

▶ lacking adequate clothing.

Poor children also have shorter lives, lower birth weight (associated with higher chance of infant death and disease), lower achievement in school, fewer qualifications and more chance of death or injury from accidents or fires (End Child Poverty, 2005). The current government sees the reduction of child poverty as a key factor in improving educational standards and creating a better workforce, and in reducing social exclusion, crime and anti-social behaviour.

Activity

Think about the impact of poverty with reference to children you work with. You might consider some of the contrasting experiences of children who live in poverty and those who have access to a wider range of resources. For example, access to a wide range of first-hand experiences such as holidays, day trips, and visiting friends and family may depend on whether the family can afford the costs. Make notes on the following questions:

▶ How does poverty affect some children?

▶ What is the impact of poverty on children's development and learning?

Discuss your ideas with colleagues or a mentor.

Political agendas

Prior to the election of the New Labour government in 1997, the long-term neglect of early years policy had resulted in early years services that were shaped as much through that neglect as by political intervention. For example, the provision of large-scale childcare by the state was seen as undesirable and thus before 1997 there was reduction rather than expansion in local authority provision. Alongside this there was a slow but escalating growth in the private and voluntary sector, with the development of adventure playgrounds and playschemes mainly by voluntary bodies, the growth of registered childminding in some areas and a very slow growth in the number of private nurseries, which began to escalate in the early 1990s.

Since 1997, the central focus of social policy has been the reduction of poverty, particularly child poverty, and early years policy has come to the forefront as a key tool to drive poverty eradication and social inclusion. Tony Blair's Beveridge lecture (March 1999; reprinted in Walker, 1999) included a pledge to eradicate child poverty within 20 years, which has subsequently been supported by a raft of new policies and legislation. Roberts (2001: 53) states that these measures are designed to 'lift around 1.2 million children out of poverty'. However, current indicators show that progress in eradicating poverty has reached a plateau and targets are unlikely to be met.

The political agenda New Labour has rolled out since 1997 is a multi-layered and complex set of strategies to reduce poverty, relieve pressure on the welfare state, raise standards in young children to improve outcomes for them as school-leavers, improve employability, reduce crime and increase social stability. This agenda has also been shaped by a distinctive philosophy influencing policy development – the emphasis on 'joined-up solutions' has been a central influence in shaping policy responses to eradicate poverty. This 'joined up' philosophy has been apparent in changes in the structure of children's services at national and local levels. A study by members and associates of the Centre for Analysis of Social Exclusion at the London School of Economics commented that the government's agenda to reduce poverty has both short-term cash and service benefits and long-term elements to improve life chances and standards for all children (Joseph Rowntree Foundation, 2005). This study also suggested that, in the short term, tax and benefits measures and reduction of unemployment had been successful in reducing child poverty for about 1.3 million children.

The New Labour political agenda has its roots in the years spent in opposition to Conservative governments between 1979 and 1997. The Labour Party went through a period of bitter rivalry between right- and left-wing factions after their defeat in 1979, leading to a left-wing leadership win and the defection of the right-wing to a new party, the Social Democrats, in 1981. Failure to win the 1983 election led to reforms in the Labour Party's philosophy and policies, which became more marked after Tony Blair was elected party leader in 1994.

Effectively, the philosophy of the 'Third Way' (as it was initially called) was developed to ensure election success for the struggling Labour Party. The main theme was an economic strategy which sought to ameliorate the worst effects of laissez-faire economic policies on the most vulnerable groups. Within this broad approach the expansion of childcare and other services for children and families has been seen in terms of its advantages to parents and the labour market, rather than in terms of children themselves. This is in contrast to other European countries where childcare is seen primarily as a service to children, reflected in state subsidy to ensure investment in high-quality staff.

Although the reduction of child poverty has driven a range of different social policy developments, the emphasis on improving conditions and outcomes for children has been a strong element of these. The trends in social development described above have led to a focus on the early years after a long period of stagnant policy development and low levels of state involvement in strategic planning and development of the early years sector, as discussed in Chapter 2.

Developments have included:

- increases in the number of childcare places to support working parents

- growth in the childcare workforce

- increased opportunities for training and gaining qualifications in the sector

- tax credits to support children and families, including those in low-paid employment

- extension of out-of-school care and extended school provision

- development of integrated service delivery.

One of the key initiatives, the National Childcare Strategy, introduced in 1998, has included a range of developments to support early years and wider policy goals. The National Childcare Strategy was also significant in flagging up the new centrality of early years in the political agenda after years of indifference. Thirty years of neglect at national policy level had left early years services in a fragmented and inadequate state, with:

- a poorly paid workforce, with limited access to training and career development for many practitioners

- service provision dominated by low levels of availability, lack of coherence between sectors and low levels of state investment

- an artificially created divide between care and education services, which meant many services failed to provide for the needs of children or parents.

Childcare policy has been aimed at some but not all of these elements of early years provision. Despite the extension of free half-day nursery places to three- and four-year-olds and the expansion of childcare places across the sectors, many working parents continue to struggle to find adequate day-long childcare that they can afford. The Childcare Act 2006 extended free places in nursery education to 15 hours a week for 38 weeks by 2010, with a further planned extension to 20 hours, but this may still not resolve the issue of affordable childcare for all families as the development of full day care has remained largely in the private day nursery sector. Childminders continue to fill the gaps but numbers have fallen and childcare places for children under three remain fewer and more expensive.

For some children, sponsored day care in a day nursery or with a childminder is available. Such places are difficult to obtain and are normally reserved for families with children in need or at risk of abuse. Local authority day nursery places, originally intended for a wider range of children, were increasingly allocated to children where there was cause for concern throughout the 1970s onwards, based on the compensatory model discussed above. Such places are now rare, but children are still funded by social care services for day nursery and childminding places where such support is seen as preventing family breakdown or the necessity of admitting a child into care.

The net result is that, despite these developments, many children's care arrangements involve a number of different settings and individuals, are vulnerable to breakdown, and deny the child coherence and consistency of care. For example, a child may be childminded between two and three years old or go to a day nursery. He/she may then continue at day nursery or go to nursery school for half a day and be cared for by relatives, friends or a childminder for the rest of the day. In some areas, nursery schools provide extended care for which parents pay. Most private day nurseries provide free nursery education so that children remain in the same setting all day, but this can be an expensive option and one not available to less well-off families, despite tax credits. For many families the options are bewildering and in choosing childcare it is no wonder that most parents do this on the basis of proximity and cost.

Yet supporting parents in their return to work is a key political agenda item. One of the main developments brought about by the New Labour government of 1997 was to bring all early years services, except those specifically to do with child welfare, within the auspices of one department, currently the Department for Children, Schools and Families (DCSF), signalling a significant change in culture as regards government policy towards supporting working parents.

The Change for Children agenda within government continues to drive developments. The publication of *Choice for Parents, the Best Start for Children: A Ten-year Strategy for Childcare* (HM Treasury et al., 2004) established the following objectives:

▶ Choice and flexibility: parents to have greater choice about balancing work and family life.

▶ Availability: for all families with children aged up to 14 who need it, an affordable, flexible, high-quality childcare place that meets their circumstances.

▶ Quality: high-quality provision with a highly skilled childcare and early years workforce, among the best in the world.

▶ Affordability: families to be able to afford flexible, high-quality childcare that is appropriate for their needs.

Specific developments planned in the Strategy and implemented in some cases through the Childcare Act 2006 included:

▶ an increase in the limits of the childcare element of Working Tax Credit

▶ the current free entitlement for three- and four-year-olds to nursery education will be extended to 12.5 hours, 38 weeks a year from 2006 and 15 hours a week by 2010 with a long-term goal of 20 hours free early education and childcare a week

▶ a Sure Start Children's Centre in every community by 2010, offering access to integrated early years activities, childcare and family services

▶ extended schools to provide a range of services and, for primary school children, a guarantee of care out of school hours and during the holidays between 8 a.m. and 6 p.m.

▶ a new duty on local authorities to secure provision of childcare, complementing authorities' existing responsibilities in relation to early education.

Activity

Talk to some parents you know through work or as friends or neighbours and/or consider your own experience of parenting and work.

▶ What issues (if any) do parents face in balancing work and childcare?

▶ What do children and parents experience on a day-to-day basis in order for parents to work?

▶ What improvements do you think the ten-year strategy may make for these families?

▶ Do you think there are any negative aspects of the early years policy for children, parents and families?

These developments signalled another phase in the current political agenda for early years policy. Policy has been largely targeted on disadvantaged areas, anti-poverty strategies and 'welfare to work'. Later developments have signalled a move towards universal (rather than targeted) early years services to meet the needs of a much wider range of children. In respect of the longer-term political agenda, these findings support the development of universal good quality early years services for children as a way of reducing intergenerational transmission of poverty and deprivation. As such, the development of early years services as outlined in the ten-year plan is central to the social inclusion agenda.

One of the influences on this development in policy may be studies by academics such as that by Peter Moss on the effectiveness of more universal early years services in other countries in meeting working parents' needs while raising educational standards. The benefits of universal early years services have been the subject of campaigns and lobbying by organizations such as the Daycare Trust for some time and there is some evidence that there is a much greater receptivity within government to these ideas as reflected in the most recent policy development. In addition, studies such as the Effective Provision of Pre-School Education (EPPE) project have confirmed the value of early years care and education to young children in terms of benefits to their learning and development (Sylva et al., 2004).

Government bodies, professional organizations and other stakeholders

One of the influences on early years policy has been the role of government agencies and professional bodies in determining developments. For example, the transfer of responsibility for early years to the DfEE from the Department of Health in 1998 was significant in signalling that early years policies were to be dominated by education in the future. In addition, the transfer of responsibility for standards and regulation from directors of social care services to Ofsted's Early Years Directorate and the creation of new responsibilities for support services in education departments in 2001 firmly placed childcare in the remit of the educationalists. The role of the Department of Health and social care services within local authorities has become much less influential in shaping policy as a result.

The combined role of the DCSF, Ofsted and the QCA has been to bring in widespread measures to standardize early years provision across the diverse sectors, with an emphasis on educational aspects of early years provision. However, these developments did have complex outcomes for some providers. Numbers of childminders had been falling since the Children Act 1989 had introduced a stricter inspection regime, and this trend continued as pressure to join formal networks and gain qualifications, together with inspections by Ofsted, impacted on the childminder's role. Between 1997 and 2000 there was a 20 per cent reduction in the childminding workforce. Many pre-schools failed to compete successfully with other providers and folded in the same time period.

The role of individuals and organizations outside government has become significant in determining policy through the work of professional organizations such as the National Children's Bureau, the Thomas Coram Research Unit, the Pre-school Learning Alliance and the National Childminding Association, to name a few. A key factor for these organizations in finding a voice in early years policy has been their strong links with government agencies, resulting in joint writing of policy and guidelines and commissioning of research from professional organizations by the DCSF. So, for example, the 2001 paper *Childcare and Early Education – Investing in All Our Futures* is a set of guidelines for local authorities to develop successful early years provision, written by the Daycare Trust for the Local Government Association (LGA) within the auspices of the DfES (DfES/LGA, 2001). Further examples of this are found in the case study of SSLPs above.

Academic institutions have also found a steady voice in early years development through their role in developing aspects of policy as well as the influence of research as discussed. For example, *Birth to Three Matters* was developed by Lesley Abbott and colleagues at Manchester Metropolitan University as a DfES-funded project in 2002 (Sure Start Unit, 2002).

One of the features of the current Labour government has been this increasing influence of professional organizations, academics and other stakeholders through their stronger links to civil servants and policy-makers. For example, the Daycare Trust has gained considerably in influence and hosts a forum for development and discussion that includes professionals, academics and policy-makers. This congruence of ideas and beliefs has been developed further through the government's emphasis on evidence-based policy-making and systematic evaluation strategies for new policies. As such, academics, research organizations and professional bodies have found a newly expanded role in policy development through government-funded research and evaluation projects. For example, the National Evaluation of Sure Start is being conducted by a group of academics led by Edward Melhuish at the Institute for the Study of Children, Families and Social Issues at Birkbeck, University of London (Melhuish et al., 2005).

The relatively recent move towards evidence-informed practice in social services, health and education has emphasized the importance of quality research and effective dissemination of findings to policy-makers and practitioners. Most recent policy developments have been based on or supported by central government-funded research programmes. The Department of Health-funded research programmes into aspects of children's welfare are one example of this. *Child Protection: Messages from Research* (Department of Health, 1995) summarized the findings of a number of studies that have had a sustained influence on policy and practice in child protection. The outcomes of the studies were significant in developments to the multi-agency child protection guidelines *Working Together to Safeguard Children* (Department of Health, 1999). Other 'messages from research' funded by the Department of Health were central to the development of adoption legislation and practice.

In early years education, studies such as the EPPE project have contributed to 'evidence-informed policy' in early years education and care (Sylva et al., 2004). The study has explored the impact of pre-school care and education on the development of children from a range of backgrounds and identified key factors in quality settings. The outcomes support the role of quality pre-schools in supporting all children's development and combating the impact of social disadvantage and special educational needs. The findings have contributed significantly towards the debate on what characteristics make high-quality pre-school provision. Seven areas related to high quality were identified relating to issues such as curriculum delivery, adult–child interactions, parental involvement and staff training and knowledge. The findings are likely to influence policy around quality in early years education for some time to come.

Evidence-informed practice is a significant development requiring individuals, organizations and policy-making bodies to support their decisions and practice with research findings. Evidence-informed findings and the outcomes of evaluation of projects are increasingly gaining a significant influence on policy development as shown in the ten-year strategy for childcare published in December 2004 (HM Treasury et al., 2004). However, it is necessary to be cautious of this approach as the contested nature of most research and the possibility of selective use of findings can impact on the value of 'evidence' as a basis for change, as discussed further in Chapter 7. Although their increased influence and involvement is generally welcome, there is a concern that the overwhelming influence of government may stifle the independent voice of professional organizations, academics and other stakeholders in the early years.

Significant events

Significant events are those that focus attention on existing failures or flaws in policy and legislation or the quality of services provided. Although these flaws and failures may already be in the public domain or part of the professional debate, key events may have a disproportionate impact as catalysts of change. Key events often draw a disproportionate amount of media attention highlighting the need for change and shaping and directing public opinion. However, they must also resonate with government agendas in order to be influential. For example, the Utting Report (Department of Health/Welsh Office, 1997), drawing on research findings mainly from the voluntary organization associated with children in care, The Who Cares? Trust, determined that children 'looked after' by local authorities (children in public care) were likely to suffer dismal outcomes in terms of education, health, employment, mental health and risk of criminality, homelessness, drug and alcohol abuse. The report was commissioned in response to widespread concerns and public outrage at the series of revelations of abuse and mistreatment of children in the public care system. The policy response was rapid and broad, introducing the Quality Protects strategy in 1998 (Department of Health, 1998), covering a range of measures to improve life chances for these children, including shorter waiting times for permanent placements, better monitoring of health and educational progress, and targets for improved educational achievements for children in care.

Some of the most significant developments currently influencing changes in the early years are the recommendations of the Green Paper *Every Child Matters* (DfES, 2003) as discussed further in Chapter 4. *Every Child Matters* was apparently published in response to the recommendations of Lord Laming's inquiry report into the death of an eight-year-old girl called Victoria Climbié, who was killed by her aunt and aunt's boyfriend in 2001 (Laming, 2003). Victoria Climbié's death brought about a sustained focus on deficits in the existing legislation and guidelines to protect children from abuse and neglect. This single case highlighted existing flaws in the management of child welfare, deficits in communications between key responsible agencies, poor quality training and lack of ability of staff to work effectively in protecting children. The sustained media interest in the case and the particularly tragic circumstances of the child's death were significant in the role that her death would take in influencing policy change. However, the influence of the Laming Report on the timing and content of *Every Child Matters* is not a simple linear relationship. Existing developments and plans within government also determined the changes and no single factor can be seen as the sole determinant of policy change.

International policy

In some ways the role of international policy development on UK policy is difficult to measure. However, there is no doubt that in recent years early years policy development in other European countries has been scrutinized and compared with that in the UK by academics such as Peter Moss and Helen Penn. It is also true that at the present time there is a strongly Europhile influence in government. In this section the influence of international policy influencing the early years is discussed in terms of its impact in the UK.

The adoption of the United Nations Convention on the Rights of the Child (UNCRC) in 1989 was a major step in establishing the rights of children as a key theme in policy development. However, within the EU there have been only limited developments in policy relating to young children, which have had only a small impact in the UK (Ruxton, 2001). This impact has partly been limited by resistance to the concept of EU intervention in the child and family policy field based on the persistent ideology of non-interventionism, which dominated UK child and family policy through the 1980s and 1990s, and by reluctance in most member states to extend the EU's influence in matters of social, as opposed to economic, policy. Areas where there has been an EU influence on family policy are in improving rights to maternity leave and restricting long hours of work.

Both of these related to economic affairs. However, Ruxton (2001: 69) argues that 'the EU has a very limited legal base for its action in relation to children'.

Despite this, there are common features of an agenda for early years policy in Europe. Moss (2001a: 28) identifies these as:

▶ a legal right to parental leave

▶ public support for the childcare needs of employed parents

▶ public support for at least two years' education for all children before they start compulsory schooling.

However, he also points out that in the UK there has only been a clear commitment to this agenda since 1997. More recently there are indications that early years policy in the UK is coming increasingly under the influence of European developments, including the move towards universal early years services and integrated planning and services delivery.

Special educational needs: a case study of accumulative influences on early years policy

Special educational needs (SEN) policy provides a good example of how a number of the influences discussed above interact to shape policy and practice. In respect of SEN, key influences on policy include:

▶ social and cultural developments in terms of how children with learning difficulties are viewed

▶ government agendas such as increasing the level of social inclusion

▶ stakeholder views such as voluntary and parent associations

▶ international policy promoting the globalization of children's rights agendas.

Before the 1980s, children with SEN were defined through medical models of disability and it was believed that many of these children could not be educated. Following an enquiry into the educational needs of children with disabilities, the Warnock Report was published in 1978 and the Education Act in 1981, establishing the concept of integration (inclusion) by legislating that children with SEN should be educated in mainstream schools if this was at all possible and that educational objectives should be the same for all children (HM Government, 2006). A proportion of children identified as having learning difficulties are given a statement of SEN, which outlines the child's needs and how these will be met. At present about 18 per cent of children in primary schools have SEN, 3 per cent of all children have statements of SEN and 1 per cent are educated in special schools.

continued

continued

Warnock (Warnock Committee, 1978) did not ignore the under-fives in the report, focusing on the following principles for supporting children in their early years with SEN:

▶ support for parents as their children's primary educators

▶ early identification and assessment of SEN and support for children under two

▶ training for all professionals involved with young children to recognize early signs of special needs and the social basis of some of these needs

▶ prompt and sensitive disclosure of disability to parents and access to information about support at an early stage

▶ a named contact for parents to provide a focus for advice and support.

The Education Act 1981 was not at the time supported by additional funding and as such it became clear that statements of SEN were subject to resource limitations from their inception, and this tension between entitlement and resource restrictions has continued as a factor as the number of children identified with SEN has risen and many special schools have closed (Croll and Moses, 2000). Muncey (1988) also critiques the Act, suggesting that it had many loopholes through which local authorities (LAs) could choose not to make significant changes to their provision.

Additional pressures on the Warnock framework arose as testing within the National Curriculum, 1988, created competition between schools, pressurizing them to focus on the children who might get good results. Moreover, in mainstream schools, 'integration' may sometimes mean segregation within the school through a number of mechanisms including specialized units for children with disabilities, some of which are highly separate from the rest of the school (Dyson, 2005).

In the Warnock Report (1978) social deprivation was not identified as a cause of SEN. However, increasingly, clusters of children with SEN are found in particular schools, settings or areas as social disadvantage, poverty and class link to higher incidences of SEN as do gender (boys) and ethnicity (Dyson, 2005). Moreover, families with children with disabilities are more likely to experience poverty as they may have restricted access to employment because of the child's needs and there may be additional expenses associated with the child's disability. This clustering creates particular problems for schools, which struggle to 'improve' in terms of conventional measured outcomes while supporting the needs of high numbers of children with SEN. As

continued

continued

more children are identified with SEN linked to social issues such as autistic spectrum disorders (ASD), the principles of inclusion are tested as settings and schools struggle to provide for children with high levels of needs. Ofsted (2006b) found that the increase in the number of children statemented for behavioural, emotional and social difficulties (BESD) meant that these children were more likely to be excluded from schools and that their inclusion was the biggest challenge to schools and settings. In the early years, too many children with emerging BESD did not get a quality response.

The Warnock Report established the principle of parent partnership to better support children with SEN, which was eventually enshrined in the Special Educational Needs Code of Practice (1993; 2001). This is a set of detailed procedures for schools, early years settings and other agencies involved in assessing and providing for children with SEN. Although parents have consistently preferred their children with SEN to be educated in mainstream schools (apart from a small number where the child has severe/complex disabilities), it is also recognized that the limitations on resources could impact negatively on successful inclusion. The concept of parent partnership in SEN is supported by the right to appeal against statementing decisions which has introduced a 'quasi-judicial element into provision for SEN' (Croll and Moses, 2000).

Since the Warnock Report, policy has continued to focus on inclusion agendas for children with learning difficulties, including children with disabilities. Policies in the UK have been influenced throughout by international developments, including the 'globalisation of rights and entitlements' for children with disabilities (Artiles and Dyson, 2005: 38). The United Nations Convention on the Rights of the Child (UNCRC) articles 12, 12 and 23 address the rights of children with disabilities in mainstream education. However, the UNCRC has been criticized for not establishing a principle that access to services according to need for disabled children should be a right (Quinn and Degener, 2002, cited in Mittler, 2005).

The United Nations Educational, Scientific, and Cultural Organization (UNESCO) Salamanca Statement on Special Needs Education, 1994, aligned the international inclusion agenda with children's rights campaigns and informed the Green Paper *Excellence for All Children: Meeting Special Educational Needs*, 1997, which linked policies in this country to international trends (Mittler, 2005).

Other policy and legislation includes:

▸ the SEN and Disability Act (SENDA), 2001, provides some protection for disabled children against discrimination in schools and confirms their right to education in mainstream schools wherever possible

continued

continued

▸ Removing Barriers to Achievement, 2004, sets out the government agenda for children with SEN within the *Every Child Matters* policy agenda focusing on early intervention; partnership with parents; inclusion and raising achievement through teacher training and monitoring progress

▸ Together from the Start (2003) and the Early Support programme focus on coordinating and raising standards for the youngest disabled children and delivering services to these children and their families through Children's Centres

▸ the Childcare Act 2006 states that LAs will only be deemed to have met the childcare needs of parents if there is sufficient provision for disabled children.

More recently, the Warnock framework has been critiqued for no longer being able to meet the needs of children with SEN, not least by Warnock herself (Warnock, 2005). Key factors under debate are the impact of inclusion on special schools closures, changed concepts of SEN now increasingly focused on social aspects of disability, and the impact of increased numbers of children with SEN in mainstream schools. In early years contexts, more children aged three and four have entered nursery education since the National Childcare Strategy started to promote increases in places in 1998. Earlier opportunity to assess young children's needs has led to many more children being identified as having SEN at an earlier stage, adding to the pressure on limited resources.

The *Statutory Assessment and Statements of SEN: In Need of Review?* (Audit Commission, 2002) suggested that statutory assessment is both slow and expensive, and ultimately may not ensure the child's needs are met due to poor levels of monitoring and geographical variations in the availability of resources. The report also found that parents struggled with statementing, finding the process stressful to go through.

The SEN policy agenda has been driven partly by international trends linked to children's rights movements and the need for government to better support all children to meet their potential and offset the high social cost of failing this group in terms of outcomes and life chances. These include higher chances of not being in education, employment or training than non-disabled young people and more likelihood of getting fewer or no qualifications. However, support for children with disabilities and SEN has also been the subject of a powerful lobby from disability charities and alliances which support a clearer inclusion agenda with political and financial backing.

Summary □

▶ The influences on early years policy are varied and have complex inter-relationships, forming systems to create particular policy developments at certain points in time.

▶ That said, policy is essentially made by governments, and the receptivity of politicians and civil servants to different views and influences on early years policy development will depend on the prevailing political agenda.

▶ At the same time, political agendas are in themselves influenced by social trends and developments, which will determine the context within which policy is framed.

Further reading 📖

Brannen, J. and Moss, P. (eds) (2003) *Rethinking Children's Care*, Buckingham: Open University Press. Part 1 contains several chapters exploring the development of childcare policy.

Pugh, G. and Duffy, B. (eds) (2006) *Contemporary Issues in the Early Years: Working Collaboratively for Children* (4th edn), London: Sage. Part One contains chapters on policy for early childhood services.

Implementing Early Years Policy

Chapter 4

This chapter discusses several issues:

▶ what is expected of policy-makers in terms of approaches to development and implementation of policy, planning and communication of policy developments, and the type of research, monitoring and evaluation activities that best support effective policy-making

▶ the implementation of policy at national, local and individual setting levels

▶ an extended case study illustrates some of the ways in which policy is implemented at the different levels and issues arising from this implementation.

The implementation of policy involves a process through which the ideas, intentions, principles and practicalities of specific policy plans and developments are made real. At national level this can be through the enactment of legislation, the development of new organizational structures or changes to existing organizations, and the transfer or alteration of responsibilities within or between local and national government. At local level this can be through the development of new local authority structures or agencies, new ways of working, and new protocols for working arrangements between agencies and other bodies such as voluntary organizations. Policy implementation can also mean new jobs and careers, new conditions of service and qualification structures within the workforce. At setting level, implementing policy may be through new organizational structures, changed or new policies, different ways of working, job descriptions and arrangements with other agencies.

Often legislation is required to pave the way for significant policy changes, but other developments take place under existing law. In the simplest terms, new policy is the result of government activity in planning and delivering implementation strategies (including legislation) for policies developed by departments and agencies. However, implementation of policy is complicated, reflecting interactions between a wide range of stakeholders in the early years including those within and outside government.

Modern policy-making

There are certain features of policy-making at the beginning of the twenty-first century that are intended to promote effectiveness and value for money. Modern policy is expected to be efficient in terms of achieving planned outcomes in a cost-effective way and not delivering any unexpected side effects that may render it ineffective or costly. Policy-making is increasingly influenced by evidence from research into the best way of achieving policy goals, and on evaluations of existing policy to determine its effectiveness. To this extent, modern policy is evidence informed and draws on lessons learned about the success or otherwise of previous policy (NAO, 2001). The government has promoted improvements in the quality of policy to try to develop long-term strategies and reduce both fragmentation in policy-making and the risks of policy either being ineffective in achieving its aims or having unforeseen negative and costly side effects.

The Centre for Management and Policy Studies in the Cabinet Office works with departments and agencies within government to help them develop skills in and approaches to effective policy-making. According to the National Audit Office there are nine characteristics of modern policy-making. It should:

▶ be forward looking

▶ be outward looking

▶ be innovative and creative

▶ use evidence

▶ be inclusive

▶ be joined up

▶ evaluate

▶ review

▶ learn lessons (NAO, 2001).

Currently, the central focus is on what policy actually achieves and this is supported by an expectation that there will be an evaluation of policy outcomes to ascertain whether policy goals have been met. This type of approach is now common in early years policy development with evaluations being conducted by academics and/or professional organizations using DCSF or other government department or agency funding. For example, the National Evaluation of Children's Trusts (NECT) was commissioned in April 2004 by the DfES and the Department of Health to evaluate the pathfinder Children's Trusts established in 2003. In line with the development of stronger links between government departments, academics and professional organizations in terms of policy development (discussed in the previous chapter), the evaluation was commissioned by the DfES and the Department of Health and conducted by academics at the University of East Anglia in conjunction with the NCB (NECT, 2004). The evaluation of the 35 Children's Trust pathfinder projects was intended to inform policy implementation, giving early messages to practitioners involved in developing integrated service delivery. Such evaluations provide information about best implementation strategies for new or emerging policy developments and legitimize these in terms of the stakeholders involved.

Modern policy-making involves ensuring new policies are considered in terms of cost, impact, risks and priorities. Policy development now requires a consideration of a range of different options for achieving policy goals, and risk and cost analyses of these in order to determine the option most likely to succeed. There are also requirements to consult with stakeholders, pilot new policies and consider their impact before extending policy developments more widely. As such, departments are required to draw up implementation plans for policy developments. These plans can include:

- a timetable for delivering policy

- roles and responsibilities for those involved in delivery

- strategies for tackling barriers to policy development

- strategies for monitoring and reporting performance

- flexible approaches (listening, monitoring, reviewing) (NAO, 2001).

The ways in which implementation plans are developed in the field of early years policy is illustrated in the case study of *Every Child Matters* (ECM) discussed below.

Activity

Find out what decisions were made in your local authority about the first wave of children's centres. Select one of the centres in that first wave and ask someone in the centre itself or in the Early Years Service in the Children's Services Department.

- Why was that location chosen for a children's centre?

- How was the base for it selected?

- What difficulties and opportunities were encountered in getting the centre going?

- What arrangements are in place for monitoring and reviewing progress?

Two other issues have become central to modern policy-making. First, using the Internet to communicate information about proposed policies, to publish policy documents, to provide a forum for debate and to conduct consultations on proposed policy. The websites of government departments and agencies and professional organizations are now major vehicles used to communicate the details of policy implementation plans and, in the case of the latter, to debate and interpret the meaning of new policy on behalf of particular audiences. Research and evaluation study reports are published on government and other websites, providing extensive information about the reasoning behind particular developments and the effectiveness of these when put into practice. Timetables for introducing new policy are published along with the consequences of policy implementation for different stakeholders including parents and children. For example, *Every Child Matters: Change for Children* is explained in a children's version on the ECM website. Practitioners now have unprecedented opportunities to access information about early years policy developments and to view and take part in the critical debate that usually accompanies such developments. However, the opportunity to contribute to a consultation does not necessarily lead to making an impact on the shape that policy will take (see Barnardos, 2003).

The 'Useful Websites' section at the end of the book gives details of the key websites for accessing this type of information in respect of early years policies and the debate around these. Individuals and organizations within the early years can use this information to keep up with policy developments in the field and to consider the impact of policy development at service delivery level within the context of their own role and/or agency.

A second issue concerns the way in which policies have increasingly been developed as 'packages' in line with the government philosophy of 'joined up' policy-making as discussed in the previous chapter. Policy-making now increasingly focuses on tackling linked issues through a range of interconnected policies. This is exemplified in the sorts of policy 'packages' that have been developed to tackle poverty and social exclusion, to promote 'welfare to work' and to improve the life chances of all children, which were discussed in the previous chapter.

The case study discussed below illustrates how the concept of 'packages' of policies has been developed in the field of early years policy in order to tackle a range of interlinked policy goals. It also demonstrates many of the other features of modern policy-making as discussed above and in particular explores the ways in which the relationships and debates between stakeholders have become crucial in determining the shape of early years policy. However, first, the stages of policy implementation are discussed.

Stages of policy implementation

In Chapter 3, we looked at the influences on policy development and how they interact to determine policy goals. Once policy goals are determined, the government has the complex job of implementing these by directing and monitoring changes at national, local and individual practice levels. The success of policy depends on the ways in which implementation plans are introduced, communicated, debated and interpreted through practice.

Green Papers

New policy is often introduced through consultation documents, called Green Papers, published by the relevant government department or agency. Originally, these contained ideas and thoughts about how policy could be developed rather than specific proposals, although this is not now always the case (see the case study below) as Green Papers tend to contain more concrete and fully formed policy proposals than previously.

In early years policy-making, consultation is usually with local authorities and the broad range of voluntary sector organizations working with children and families and research institutes in the field. Organizations and individuals will send their written responses to the relevant government department or agency, and such responses are usually published on the Internet by the organizations involved. The extent to which consultation responses influence government plans can vary and tends to depend on the confidence the government has in implementing their plans successfully, the extent to which there is general acceptance of those plans, the anticipated difficulties of implementing policy at local level and whether the proposed amendments will change the basic structure of new policy.

White Papers

Once the consultation process is completed, the government may draw up a more specific report containing concrete proposals for policy developments called a White Paper. White Papers 'signify a clear intention on the part of a government to pass new law' (TheyWorkForYou.com, 2005). A White Paper is not generally a consultation document although it may promote discussion about the detail of new legislation. A White Paper normally leads to the introduction of a bill, which is a draft new law. Not all policy requires legislation to implement it as discussed in the case study below.

Effectively, a Bill travels in a predetermined process through Parliament as outlined in Figure 4.1. The stages of parliamentary process are designed to ensure that there is time for considered debate about all aspects of the legislation, for amendments to be tabled and discussed, agreed or disagreed, and for scrutiny by relevant bodies and committees to ensure that the legislation is robust and not fatally flawed. In the case of large, complex or very influential bills, progress through Parliament will be scrutinized by the media and concerned organizations.

Understanding Early Years Policy

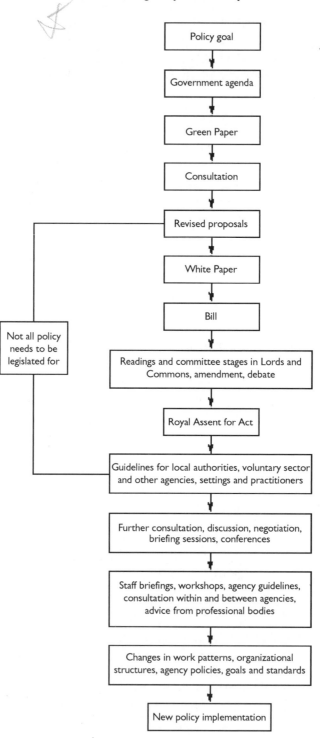

Figure 4.1 *Stages of policy implementation for the early years*

Act of Parliament

After the final stage, Royal Assent, when a bill becomes law it is known as an Act. There is a gap in time before the Act is implemented as often it requires changes in the way services are organized or delivered. For example, in the case of the Children Act 1989, implementation took place over a two-year period. This time is used to interpret the legislation at local and national levels and to put in place policies and structures, including financial measures, to ensure that the legislation can be successfully implemented.

The process may then involve intense activity on the part of government to issue guidelines and information about how to implement the policy or legislation at local level if this is required. This may include briefings and conferences, written advisory documents and meetings with key local government bodies. Within local authorities information about expected changes will be disseminated through staff briefings, invitations to stakeholders to consult, and workshops to debate and plan with those stakeholders.

Implementing the proposals in *Every Child Matters*

The implementation of *Every Child Matters* is discussed as an extended case study of how policy affecting early years is put into practice at different levels. The discussion includes looking at the roles of different national and local organizations in ensuring implementation, how expectations are disseminated to local level, and the role of national and local government officers and professional bodies in developing and establishing implementation plans. Finally, the impact on different sectors of the workforce is discussed in the light of the range of changes to structures and work practices.

Implementation at national government level

The Green Paper *Every Child Matters* (DfES, 2003) incorporated a raft of policy proposals, which effectively extended and continued the drive towards integrated service planning and delivery for children and families. As discussed in Chapter 3, the impetus for this particular raft of policy developments came from the recommendations of the Laming Report into Victoria Climbié's death, although this single event acted as a catalyst for putting planned government policy into place rather than as the sole reason for policy change. To a large extent, the Green Paper was intended to extend existing policy plans further. However, new policy principles were also introduced, with a shift from focusing mainly on areas of disadvantage to include more emphasis on universal services to all children. As with a great deal of policy impacting on the early years, the recommendations of the Green Paper covered a wider range of policy areas including family and youth justice. However, changes to how young children are supported and protected are key elements of the developments.

One of the key influences on the development of the Green Paper was the Inter-Agency Group (IAG). Formed in 2002 in response to issues arising from the Laming Report, the IAG is a group of representatives from key agencies in children's services such as local authority directors' organizations in education and social services, for example, the Association of Directors of Education and Children's Services, and children's charities, for example, Barnardos, National Society for the Prevention of Cruelty to Children (NSPCC) and National Children's Home (NCH). Originally convened by the President of the Association of Directors of Social Services (ADSS), the group have met since 2002, becoming influential in their advice to government on issues arising from the Laming Report, including the Green Paper. One of the main outcomes of the group has been to bring together the views of the statutory and voluntary sectors and to convey these views to policy-makers in central government through their contacts with ministers, such as the Children's Minister, and senior civil servants in the DfES.

One of the main issues at national level was the need to 'join up Whitehall' and create much more cohesive planning for children's services between the DfES, the Department of Health and the Home Office (Waterman and Fowler, 2004). The Children's Minister post was established in mid-2003 along with a new sector within the DfES – the Children, Young People and Families Directorate – providing a focus for integrating children's and families' services within central government and bringing together responsibility for:

▶ children's social care

▶ childcare and pre-school support

▶ careers advice

▶ family support

▶ legal services (Waterman and Fowler, 2004).

In addition, the establishment of the Sure Start Unit within the DfES in 2002 was a significant step in establishing an integrated approach to policy development within the government. This is reflected in the confidence with which cross-departmental issues are handled within the proposals.

The Green Paper, published in September 2003, set out a range of recommendations for changes in the way that children's welfare and progress are supported. A Green Paper is basically a consultation document, setting out intended changes and inviting comment on these. One definition of a Green

Paper is a 'tentative report of British government proposals without any commitment to action' (TheyWorkForYou.com, 2005). However, this Green Paper varied from this norm in that there was little that was tentative about the report. This is discussed in more detail below.

Key aims of the Green Paper included:

▸ linking child protection services to universal services for all children

▸ tackling chronic problems of poor communication and information sharing between services for children

▸ strengthening accountability and management of services to children

▸ developing a better trained children's workforce

▸ integrating efforts to support children's welfare with those to develop children's potential.

These aims were clearly placed in the context of existing government policy to tackle poverty and social exclusion for children and families.

The Green Paper also stated that changes were to be focused on four key areas:

▸ supporting parents and carers

▸ early intervention and effective protection

▸ accountability and integration of services

▸ workforce reforms.

Key developments proposed were:

▸ creating Children's Centres across the country, initially in the 20 per cent most deprived wards

▸ promoting full-service extended schools

▸ funding to increase out-of-school activities

▸ funding to extend Child and Adolescent Mental Health Services (CAMHS)

▸ extending speech therapy services

▸ tackling homelessness

▸ reforming the youth justice system.

Within these proposals some specific developments were identified that would bring about changes to early years service provision. One of the key themes within these proposed changes is that of integration of service delivery. In a sense, this concept came out of the perceived failure of different children's services to work effectively together to ensure children's safety and welfare.

This message is not new. Although it was a central finding of the Victoria Climbié inquiry, it was also a central finding of many previous child death inquiries including Jasmine Beckford's and Kimberley Carlile's in the 1980s. Some of the specific developments proposed included:

▶ removing barriers to information sharing between services

▶ ensuring each child/family had a lead professional responsible for co-ordinating and monitoring service delivery

▶ developing schools and Children's Centres as delivery points for a wide range of services to improve the speed and efficiency of the response to identified need.

In order to achieve new levels of accountability and to integrate services a number of structural changes at local authority level were proposed:

▶ new Directors of Children's Services for integrated education and children's social care services

▶ development of Children's Trusts to include some children's health services and other relevant agencies

▶ a lead council member for children

▶ replacing Area Child Protection Committees (ACPCs) with Local Safeguarding Children Boards.

At national level proposals included:

▶ a Minister for Young People, Children and Families

▶ a Children's Commissioner

▶ workforce reform including a common qualifications framework and training routes for those working with children and a Children's Workforce Unit in the DfES.

The Green Paper was the subject of widespread attention among those involved in children's services and within the media, with a large number of organizations commenting on and publishing their responses to the proposals. The breadth of the debate was described as 'unprecedented' in the follow-up document *Every Child Matters: Next Steps* (DfES, 2004a). The debate was supported and promoted through a series of regional conferences to brief stakeholders about the proposals and provide a forum for discussion. In addition to the Green Paper itself, a children's and young people's version was disseminated and consultation groups set up to get the views of a sample. Altogether, 1,500 adults and 3,100 young people responded to the consultation exercise. However, Barnardos queried whether their extensive consultation with children and young people actually influenced the outcomes at all (Barnardos, 2003).

In March 2004, the paper *Every Child Matters: Next Steps* was published, summarizing this response to the Green Paper and coinciding with the introduction into Parliament of the Children Bill. *Next Steps* included:

▶ an explanation of the proposals within the Children Bill

▶ an explanation of the aspects of change which did not require legislation

▶ the outcomes of the consultation process.

The consultation endorsed the government's proposals within the Green Paper to a great extent, both supporting the principles underpinning the changes and the practical measures suggested. However, there were a number of areas where concerns were expressed, particularly around the issues of resourcing the proposals, ensuring all stakeholders were fully involved and ensuring that local flexibility was maintained in delivering integrated services. More specifically, these included:

▶ the extent to which all stakeholders, especially voluntary and community sector organizations, were involved in the developments

▶ the lack of clarity about the role of the Director of Children's Services and Children's Trusts and whether this model would be flexible to meet the requirements of all localities

▶ whether there would be sufficient funding and resources to support the developments in local authorities

▶ whether the role of the Children's Commissioner in England would be sufficiently robust.

The agencies expressing most concerns were voluntary sector organizations anxious to clarify their role in the new integrated local structures. Within the Green Paper there was a lack of detail about how these agencies would be included in the new structures and whether they would be adequately represented in planning. Proposals to merge local authority departments clearly signalled the key role of local authorities in planning and service delivery but left some concerned that other agencies such as health and the police may be marginalized.

At local government level the response to the Green Paper demonstrated some concerns about implementation strategies. The Local Government Association (LGA, 2004) urged that implementation of the Green Paper plans should take place within a framework of flexible options for structural changes within local authorities. The LGA emphasized that local authorities should have the flexibility and freedom to choose how they proceeded with integrating service planning and provision. This was echoed within debates about implementation within some local authorities. In particular, the emphasis on Children's Trusts as the only way forward was not accepted by all.

The Children's Commissioner role caused some particular concerns because it seemed to be couched in vague terms that left many questions about what the powers of the Commissioner in England might be. For example, the Commissioner has a role in involving children and gaining their views, but only a very restricted role in reviewing individual children's cases. This is in contrast to the Welsh Commissioner who has more extensive powers, for example to request and get information. The Children's Minister claimed that the vagueness surrounding the role in the Green Paper was because of the need for further consideration of the Children's Commissioner role. What is unclear is why the Commissioner for England's role still needed further consideration when the role of the Welsh Commissioner has been providing a model for several years.

The media focused to a considerable extent on plans to introduce a ban on smacking within the Children Bill. The long-running and periodically heated debate about banning smacking of children in line with many other European countries was resurrected by these proposals and this drew media attention more noticeably than any other aspect of the proposals. The strong pro-smacking lobby campaigned successfully to reduce the impact of the proposals, despite a rebellion by 47 Labour backbench Members of Parliament who voted for an outright ban.

The outcome was a compromise that satisfied neither the anti-smacking children's rights lobby nor the pro-smacking organizations. While the changes got rid of the contentious provision in previous legislation that some physical abuse of children could be defended on the grounds of 'reasonable chastisement', this does not constitute a total ban on smacking as lobbied for by organizations such as 'Children are Unbeatable!'. Instead a compromise was pushed through that continued to allow mild forms of physical punishment within the law, but outlawed forms of punishment that caused visible bruising or mental harm to the child. The government has avoided addressing the smacking issue for a substantial time. It is likely that this is in response to its concerns about the possible electoral losses associated with a firm and outright ban.

The media also tapped into concerns about the ethics of the proposed electronic data sharing between agencies. These concerns focused on the need to review both the Human Rights Act and the Data Protection Act to allow for data sharing to take place. Lack of detail about the safeguards around privacy and confidentiality and concerns about the impact on children's rights were central to this debate.

Normally, the next step after a Green Paper would have been to publish a White Paper, as discussed earlier in this chapter. However, in this case the government took the unusual step of drawing up the Children Bill, missing out the White Paper stage. This decision may have been taken to ensure speed in implementing the policy developments, but in some senses it may have been because the *Every Child Matters* Green Paper was much more detailed and specific in its provisions than Green Papers usually are. There is also speculation from some quarters that the government's haste was due to concerns that further tragedies might occur before new policy was in place to protect children. The decision to miss out on a White Paper caused some unease in that there were fears that certain aspects of the proposals may be legislated on before they were fully developed, for example the role of the Children's Commissioner, as discussed above.

Although ostensibly a consultation document, *Every Child Matters* was largely a finished product, detailing proposed policy changes which have mainly survived the consultation stage with few changes. It was clear that the government was determined to take forward their plans rapidly and with few concessions to those who were involved in the wider consultation. Despite the significant level of response to the Paper, no major changes were made to the original proposals, which raises questions about the purposes of the consultation process.

The provisions of the Children Bill were also outlined in *Every Child Matters: Next Steps* and discussed in relation to the outcomes of the consultation. The Children Bill included areas where policy change needed to be facilitated by legislative change. Not all aspects of policy change require legislation to implement, but where there are existing laws facilitating policy, legislation may be needed to allow change to take place. Some of the areas where legislation was needed to bring about the changes outlined in *Every Child Matters* are:

▸ introducing a Children's Commissioner for England responsible for promoting the views and interests of children within and outside Parliament

▸ outlining the functions of Children's Commissioners in Wales, Scotland and Northern Ireland

▸ requiring local authorities to make arrangements to work in partnership with other agencies, particularly with the voluntary and community sectors

▸ setting up Local Safeguarding Children Boards to monitor and direct multi-disciplinary child protection work

▸ establishing the role of Director of Children's Services within every local authority

▸ an integrated inspection regime covering a wide range of children's services headed by Ofsted

▸ a lead council member for children in each local authority.

Interestingly, although the bill contained clauses about encouraging and facilitating the development of Children's Trusts, the development of these was not made statutory. The Children Act 2004 included enabling clauses that laid down the legal basis for establishing Children's Trusts. As such, the role of Children's Trusts was clarified in terms of their key function of pooling budgets, staff, services and other resources to provide more integrated services but, despite the government's expectations that all authorities will eventually establish trusts, they are not specified as such in the Act. This meant that the provision of the Act allowed for more flexibility at local authority level as to how they will organize children's services than was initially anticipated (Ashrof, 2005).

The passage of the Children Bill through Parliament was turbulent, taking nine months, and being characterized by the tabling of amendments and re-amendments as a 'tug of war' took place between the Lords and Commons over some of the more controversial parts of the bill. The main disappointments for children's charities and agencies were the compromises or decisions made about the information databases, the smacking ban and the role of the Children's Commissioner for England (*Community Care*, 2004).

The information database remained an issue after the Act was passed, partly because of initial lack of clarity about how it would work. It was decided that children who receive any mainstream services would be on the database, which effectively meant the majority of children, as most receive services from primary care trusts (PCTs). Concerns at the time included the replacement of the locally based Child Protection Registers with the national database (now named ContactPoint), which could lead to vital information about children who may be abused getting lost in a much bigger pool of information. The database was to include details such as name, address, gender, date of birth, parent details and information about professionals working with the child. Some concerns were based on the Civil Service's poor track record in introducing major information and communications technology (ICT) systems.

Activity

Ask several parents about their views on the introduction of ContactPoint.

▶ Do they feel happy about a range of professionals having access to information about their children?

▶ What sort of controls do they think should be in place to protect confidentiality? Do parents know the reasons for having the database?

▶ What are the benefits and risks to children associated with the database?

Collate your answers and discuss with colleagues or a mentor.

The Education Select Committee's inquiry into the government's child welfare reform strategy reported that the proposed database was too complicated and much too costly to be feasible. One expert witness, Richard Thomas, pointed out that a database of 11 million children could make it more, not less, difficult to identify problems and issues for individuals. This issue highlights some of the problems created by the volume and range of provisions within the Green Paper and the difficulties of progressing the strategy on a multitude of fronts simultaneously. Implementation of electronic data-sharing is discussed further below.

As discussed above, the role of the Children's Commissioner, which had been questioned at the Green Paper stage particularly by voluntary sector organizations, was the cause of some of the turbulence. Children's rights groups such as the Children's Rights Alliance wanted the Children's Commissioner to have a role in supporting and developing children's rights issues and safeguarding children's rights. They wanted the Children's Commissioner to have a much wider remit to investigate cases, like the Commissioners in Wales, Scotland and Northern Ireland. However, there was strong opposition to this approach from Margaret Hodge, the then Children's Minister, and Baroness Ashton, Minister for Sure Start, and with a few minor concessions their view prevailed, despite an initial defeat in the House of Lords. This opposition to a rights-based role seemed to be based on the view that in such a role the Commissioner would get bogged down in individual cases (*Community Care*, 2004).

The outcome disappointed many children's agencies and children's rights groups with concerns that the Children's Commissioner for England has a weak role with fewer powers than his counterparts elsewhere in the UK and Europe. There were also concerns about the role of the Commissioner for England for non-devolved matters in Wales and reserved matters in Scotland, which could lead to confusion about responsibilities in some areas.

The Children Bill became law as the Children Act 2004, paving the way for the changes outlined above. The key focus of the Act was enabling rather than prescribing change, allowing local authorities flexibility in how they implemented the proposals. Other changes that have not required legislation were detailed in *Every Child Matters: Change for Children* (DfES, 2004b) as discussed above.

Implementation at regional and local level

One thing that was clear from the start of the implementation of the *Every Child Matters* strategy is that local authorities were in line for the bulk of the structural and cultural change and that this would take place mainly within existing budgets. Although the strategy was influenced by and largely welcome to the Inter-Agency Group (IAG), representing key organizations involved in the implementation, this did not detract from the overwhelming scale of the task. Central government provided a massive amount of guidance and information to support this process.

One of the central features of the implementation of the Green Paper proposals was the extent of information made available to support the changes. The government website www.everychildmatters.gov.uk has been a central resource for disseminating the ethos and principles of the reforms and detailing what is expected of local authorities and other key agencies to ensure the changes are made. Local authorities and other key agencies have been advised by documents outlining their roles and the deadlines for achieving each phase of change under the general heading of *Every Child Matters: Change for Children*. This information has been accompanied by a timetable for implementing changes, which includes deadlines for the issue of guidelines and introduction of:

▸ a duty for agencies to cooperate with each other

▸ integrated services (Children's Trusts)

▸ an integrated Children's and Young Person's Plan

▸ a Director of Children's Services in each local authority

▸ a lead member for children's services in each local council

▸ an integrated inspection framework.

Support at regional level came largely through the appointment of regional change advisers to support local developments with a budget of £20 million. Change was initially particularly focused on the development of Children's Trusts and co-located teams. Typically, within local authorities there were staff briefings to provide information about the planned new structures, invitations to consult and workshops on inter-agency aspects of change. Bodies within local government involved in such discussions included ACPCs and strategic planning groups.

It may seem that the implementation of the strategy was well coordinated and informed, leading to smooth transitions. However, there were a number of major concerns about the implementation of the strategy at service provision level. Implementing large, complex policy packages like *Every Child Matters: Change for Children*, which requires significant structural and cultural changes across a range of professional groups and agencies, is a major challenge to local authorities. One issue, which is not uncommon in policy implementation of any sort, is the budget local authorities have had to bring about the changes. Local authorities were advised by Margaret Hodge to be smarter with their money when asking for more. The budget for change at local authority level was £22 million in 2006/07 and £63 million in 2007/08. This was not considered enough by local authorities and there was a view that it may limit the effectiveness of the implementation: 'Observers feared the limited funds meant that the Act would meet the same fate as the Children Act, 1989, which was regarded as a sound piece of legislation that didn't fulfil its expectations as a result of lack of funding' (Ashrof, 2005: 1).

Another issue is the range of problems associated with 'introducing innovative programmes into mainstream services' (Dawson, 2004: 24). Although local authorities had more flexibility to do this than initially anticipated, to achieve these changes required massive cultural and structural change. Local authorities had the responsibility of addressing structural change and how this would be achieved (a significant problem in itself), but there was very little said at central government level about the cultural change required to make integrated services work. It was anticipated that there would be both institutional and personal resistance to change among the workforce in the face of new regimes, new management structures, new ways of working and new cultures.

The emphasis on structural change may mask the need for cultural change as different workforces with their own ways of working, goals and motivations, philosophies and work practices come together. One concern was that the government simply failed to recognize the enormity of the transition required within local government to successfully integrate services. Multi-disciplinary teams were hardly a new concept, but evidence shows that many are left to cope with 'complex and unforeseen challenges' including different training, jargon, priorities, world views and working traditions (Rickford, 2005). Frost (2005) and his colleagues researched the work of several multi-agency teams to explore the issues and challenges in successful integration. He determined that the teams faced challenges in the following areas:

▶ structural

▶ ideological

▶ procedural

▶ inter-professional.

Frost found that teams either worked towards conflict resolution or conflict avoidance and that having another external agency (a common enemy?) to work against was effective in achieving better integration. He concluded that factors for success were:

▶ appropriate structures and systems, for example, co-location

▶ shared professional beliefs and ideologies

▶ time for professional knowledge sharing

▶ active learning contexts.

The Children's Workforce Development Council (CWDC) was established to support workforce developments to achieve the goals of the *Every Child Matters: Change for Children* strategy. One of its roles is to ensure a common culture between different sectors is developed. However, it is clear that to achieve cultural change takes time and effort and is not achievable through merely making structural changes. As Dame Denise Platt, Chair of the Commission for Social Care Inspection, said at the 2004 Inter-Agency Group Conference: 'In practice, integration too often means new boundaries around old behaviours' (Platt, 2004).

Points for reflection 〰

▸ Consider the last time you worked with or had contact with practitioners/professionals from another disciplinary background or agency.

▸ Were there any areas of difference in your view of the work you were doing, for example, the needs of a child and family?

▸ Did you focus on the same issues or have different ideas about what was important?

▸ Were your goals the same?

▸ Think about how comfortable you felt working with someone from a different professional background.

Cultural and structural change mean different things for different sections of the workforce. Social care services workers have been concerned that they will be overwhelmed by education and health as their separate departmental bases disappear. This view may be exacerbated by the continuing lead that education takes in the development of children's services. In 2005, 50 per cent of Directors of Children's Services took up their posts and 90 per cent of these were former Chief Education Officers (CEOs) rather than Directors of Social Services or other senior positions in children and family services (Hunter, 2005). It is widely acknowledged that ex-CEOs have a steep learning curve in areas normally firmly within the remit of children's social care services, such as providing statutory child protection services. Chief Education Officers generally lack understanding or experience of safeguarding children and this lack could be dangerous for children (*Community Care*, 2005). Concerns focused around the possibility that changes that impacted more on social care services than education underestimated the cultural differences between them. This in turn led to concerns about the destabilization of ongoing services to children and families during the transition period and whether child protection services would be at risk in the longer run (ADSS, 2005; Waterman and Fowler, 2004). While it is difficult to assess the extent to which these issues remain as concerns, Gillen (2008) evaluates progress towards Laming's recommendations five years on and among other findings suggests that introducing Directors of Children's Services has probably not improved accountability for safeguarding children.

Other concerns expressed by the Association of Directors of Social Services

(ADSS) during the early stages of implementing Change for Children included the emphasis on co-location of staff and whether this had become a goal in itself rather than a means of delivering effective multi-agency services to children and families. Also, their report highlighted the fact that while other agencies had a duty to cooperate in the delivery of integrated services, Directors of Children's Services had no powers to make them fulfil this duty (ADSS, 2005).

It is clear that local authorities have had to find their own ways to implement the changes within the hard-won boundaries of flexibility agreed by central government and within the requirements of a rapid implementation timetable. This has meant that the changes have been implemented at different rates between local authorities, with some lagging behind and mixed progress (Jackson, 2005). Jackson highlights the different approaches to development of pathfinder Children's Trusts within two authorities to demonstrate the diversity of approaches and argues that the developments are not about 'bricks and mortar' but about finding ways of working in partnership that work within the particular context. There is no single approach to integration that will work in every context.

Concerns have been expressed about the rate of progress overall in terms of the effectiveness of the ECM agenda. Lord Laming was reported as stating that good practice could have prevented child deaths subsequent to Victoria Climbié's, implying that this was not yet universal. The report suggested that the pace of change in putting Laming's recommendations into place was too slow in some areas (BBC, 2008a). The conclusion is inevitable – overcoming barriers between professionals trained to think their way of working is best is taking time to achieve and involves massive cultural and structural change.

The current focus on integration within local authorities may result in some of the issues that arise from further integration with other agencies, such as health and voluntary services for children, becoming a secondary consideration. The emphasis on local authority leadership and the role of Children's Trusts may divert efforts from developing the wider partnerships that would more closely involve these agencies.

Implementing the Common Assessment Framework, Lead Professional and Information Sharing Index (ContactPoint)

In this section of the extended case study, the introduction of specific strategies to support aspects of Change for Children is explored in order to examine some of the issues of implementation in more detail. A key element of the *Every Child Matters: Change for Children* agenda is ensuring that access to specific services for children with additional needs is embedded in universal services for all children.

The Laming Report (2003) identified poor coordination between services, failure to share information and lack of professional cooperation as key elements contributing to the death of Victoria Climbié at the hands of her carers. However, other child death inquiries going back over several decades also identified similar aspects of multi-agency service provision as problematical in terms of effective safeguarding. Other vulnerable groups such as 'looked-after' children and children with disabilities have also experienced deficits in service delivery due to poor integration of different professional/agency involvement. In addition, many children waited for unacceptable lengths of time for services to be provided as they went through serial assessments as a result of intra- or inter-agency referral. Children with disabilities, who may receive services from health, education, voluntary sector and social care services were often particularly subject to multiple assessments and uncoordinated services.

Case study – Donny

Donny was 6 years old when his school decided to explore the possibility that he had a specific learning disability, after a six-month period of discussions with his parents about their concerns, and in-class assessment by his teacher. Donny was assessed by an LA advice teacher three months later, who then referred him for assessment by an educational psychologist as she thought he might be dyslexic. Nine months later, Donny was assessed by the educational psychologist. However, in the meantime his parents had asked for a full paediatric assessment through children's health services because of the long wait and Donny's increasing frustration in school, which was affecting his behaviour. The educational psychologist identified that Donny was dyslexic a month before the full paediatric assessment confirmed this and suggested he was also dyspraxic. A year and a half after concerns about his learning ability had arisen (a quarter of his whole life and nearly two school years) Donny still had not received any services to support his learning or development.

The Common Assessment Framework (CAF), lead professional and information sharing index (ContactPoint) are cornerstones of the strategy to embed safeguarding and support for children with additional needs within universal service provision. Key principles of the strategy are to:

▶ reduce the number of assessments children with additional needs are subject to in order to simplify assessment, reduce stress on the child and family, make good use of resources and speed up the delivery of services to meet need

▶ ensure that services delivered by more than one professional agency to the same child/family are appropriately coordinated to reduce overlap and gaps in service provision and to improve accountability

▶ ensure that professionals are aware of other agencies involved with a child/family to improve coordination of service delivery and to provide opportunities for professionals to share information about any concerns about a child with involved others.

Common Assessment Framework

The CAF is an initial assessment process, which can be used by any front-line children's services professional, to provide an assessment of a child and family where additional needs are identified in terms of outcomes for the child. Assessment focuses on all aspects of the child's development, the environment and on parenting capacity. It is positive in that it focuses on areas where need is met as well as those where more support is required. For some children, specialist assessments will be needed in addition and the CAF may act as a referral for these.

The use of the CAF offers the opportunity to accelerate and simplify the assessment process so that children have fewer assessments and less waiting time for services to be introduced. The CAF is designed for use in consultation with families and children and, as it is a voluntary process, they can refuse to be assessed.

Common Assessment Frameworks are often introduced after a pre-assessment checklist has been used to identify the possibility of additional needs. Common Assessment Frameworks are not just used to assess – part of the process is to identify and secure relevant resources to improve outcomes for the child. However, CAFs do not replace safeguarding processes and procedures where child protection concerns are the key issue.

The initial introduction of the CAF has been evaluated by Brandon et al. (2006) who found:

▶ in general the CAF has been welcome, although the initial introduction took longer than expected

▶ the purpose of the CAF was sometimes misunderstood and sometimes it was used just as a referral tool rather than as an assessment

▶ the time that CAFs took to complete was seen as adding to workloads, and some professionals found the forms difficult to complete

▶ there were different levels of understanding of this type of assessment between professional groups, depending on previous experience, with health and social care staff more likely to understand holistic assessment than education staff

▶ parental involvement with the CAF was not always fully understood and staff were not always clear about parents' rights to refuse to be involved.

The Lead Professional role

While the coordination of inter-agency services through one professional is not a new concept, the introduction of a lead professional (LP) has ensured a much more universal approach to this. The purposes of the role are to ensure that services are delivered effectively and efficiently to families, minimizing overlap and ensuring service provision is seamless. The lead professional also may reduce stress on families involved with a number of agencies by providing a single contact point for them. Sloper (2004) found that families with children with disabilities benefited from and welcomed having a single professional responsible for coordinating their often complex multi-agency services.

In their evaluation, Brandon et al. (2006) found that there were some concerns among professionals about performing this role, linked to lack of previous professional experience. These included:

▶ anxiety around taking on new roles

▶ concerns about the high level of responsibility in the role

▶ different concepts of the main purpose of the role.

Lead professionals need skills to work with families and other professionals, and these vary between different disciplines and levels of worker. Issues of whether particular staff are paid to take on this leadership role, whether they have appropriate skills and the time to do the role have been raised as the role has been introduced.

However, Brandon et al. (2006) identified a range of benefits to parents from introducing the lead professional role, including swifter outcomes for families and better communication between agencies and families.

The study also identified key factors for successful implementation of CAF and the lead professional including:

▶ Enthusiasm at grass roots and managerial level

▶ History of good multi-agency working and practice

▶ Clear structure for CAF/LP process

▶ Perceived benefits for families

▸ Good support, training, supervision, guidance

▸ Learning from others.
  Brandon et al. (2006: 10):

And for poorer results:

▸ Mismatch between the 'vision' and the practice

▸ Lack of agency join up – conflicts of interest

▸ Lack of professional trust

▸ Anxiety about increased workload

▸ Gaps in skill and confidence

▸ Confusion and muddle about CAF/LP processes

▸ Lack of support.
  Brandon et al. (2006: 11)

Successful implementation could be achieved more effectively through a top-down approach including a 'clear strategy' linked to local guidance and awareness raising, a phased roll-out and multi-agency training including managers, and an effective information technology (IT) system (adapted from Brandon et al. 2006: 11).

One of the main criticisms of the CAF and lead professional roll-out was that the training was not sufficient to ensure confidence in using CAFs and taking the lead professional role among all sectors of the children's workforce. Brandon et al. (2006) concluded that training needed to be ongoing rather than one-off and that more managers needed to be trained to ensure that new approaches to work required to effectively embed the CAF and lead professional were adopted.

Information Sharing Index (ContactPoint)

Sharing of information between agencies involved with a child through a national database was recommended in the Laming Report, leading to trail-blazers in a number of authorities to test and evaluate the feasibility of such a database (2003). The resulting information sharing index, ContactPoint, links up already established local databases and holds basic information about children up to the age of 18, and with their permission, care-leavers and children with learning difficulties, until they are 25. The information held is restricted by the Children Act 2004 and does not include any assessment information. The main additional information relates to details of professionals and agencies involved with the child and family, including health and education services.

These details also include whether there is a lead professional and who this is, and whether a CAF has been completed in respect of the child.

The purpose of ContactPoint is for professionals involved with a child and family to be aware of other agencies and professionals who are also working with them. This is aimed at aiding rapid and effective inter-professional cooperation and ensuring better information sharing than previously. The resource implications are also outlined in terms of professional hours 'lost' trying to track others involved with a child and family (ECM, 2008).

Reservations about the proposed database were voiced from rights groups and others from when the Children Bill was going through Parliament, focusing on concerns about privacy and rights, unauthorized access that could put children at more risk, the complexity and possible technical difficulties of a database this size, and a possible 'labelling' factor where contact with particular services could shape views of a child for years to come. The Association of Directors of Children's Services were reported to be concerned about the possibility of abusers getting access to the database because it is not clear who has responsibility for vetting the 330,000 authorized users. In addition, the fact that children of politicians and celebrities may be 'shielded' (their details guarded or left out) seemed to imply that the safety of the system cannot be guaranteed (Elliott, 2007). This is supported by a DCSF-commissioned report published by Deloitte and Touche (2008) which: 'identified "a significant risk" to ContactPoint from the security procedures of local councils and other organisations accessing the database' (BBC, 2008b). However, the proposed benefits of ContactPoint were largely supported by the evaluation of the local trailblazers, which found that the databases did link involved agencies more quickly and that this had a positive effect on the speed of intervention (Cleaver et al., 2004).

The introduction of the CAF and the lead professional, while generally welcome, has posed challenges in terms of implementation because of the new processes and ways of working demanded. Local authorities have been more effective where they have provided a clear lead on implementation as opposed to a less successful bottom-up approach. Training has been criticized where it has been seen as a 'one-off' rather than an ongoing process for all staff and managers. However, improvements and increasing use of the processes imply that early difficulties may be overcome if authorities can learn from each other's experience. The challenges of implementing ContactPoint have been different, focusing on issues about the impact on children's rights in terms of privacy, technical problems and the safety of a national database accessed by a large number of users. Concerns are ongoing at the time of writing and the longer-term success of ContactPoint remains under debate.

Summary ☐

The implementation of the *Every Child Matters: Change for Children* programme is part of much broader policy developments that include the aims of the National Health Framework and the provisions of the Childcare Act 2006, designed to make widespread changes to the ways that mainstream and specialist services are delivered to children.

The extended case study highlights the complex processes by which policy is developed and implemented and the key stages in this process. It also highlights the roles of different bodies and individuals, emphasizing that policy-making and implementation is essentially a human activity with all the unpredictability and flawed nature of human activities. Despite the apparently rational nature of the processes involved, policy plans are put into action by a process of negotiation between bodies with different levels of power and influence. In this case, government plans have survived the process largely unscathed and, despite the many ongoing concerns, there is a general climate for change and consensus about the broad direction this should take.

Key factors in implementing the strategy within *Every Child Matters: Change for Children* were:

▸ the role of key ministers and civil servants within newly integrated central government bodies, which reflected a strong commitment to improving children's welfare services

▸ the complex and ongoing interactions between these ministers and senior civil servants and representatives of the voluntary sector and local and regional bodies and bodies such as IAG

▸ the media role in highlighting particular issues for attention

▸ the government's success in defeating or reversing key amendments as the Children Bill passed through Parliament

▸ placing local authorities at the centre of implementation of the strategy.

However, the strategy is large and detailed and many issues remain to be resolved in implementing it effectively, including successfully promoting cultural change to support integrated teamwork and ensuring that partnership is successful with the range of organizations and agencies outside local government Children's services departments.

Further reading

Waterman, C. and Fowler, J. (2004) *Plain Guide to the Children Act, 2004*, Slough: NFER. Contains an annotated copy of the Act with a useful preliminary discussion explaining aspects of the legislation and how it was developed. The annotations explain the meanings of different parts of the Act.

Keeping up to date with new early years policy means reading magazines such as *Nursery World* and *Community Care* and newspapers such as the *Guardian* and the *Independent* – all of which can also be found online.

The main government websites for following early years policy developments and key documents are listed at the end of the book.

Early Years Policy in Wales, Scotland and Northern Ireland: The Impact of Devolution

Chapter 5

This chapter describes:

▶ the structure of devolved government that has developed in the UK since 1997

▶ the development of early years policy under the devolved regimes in Wales, Scotland and Northern Ireland

▶ the impact that devolution has had on the development of early years policy across the UK

▶ the potential value of comparisons of policy within the UK.

Devolution and policy-making

The UK is dominated in several senses by England, the country whose population constitutes more than 80 per cent of that of the kingdom as a whole and whose largest city, London, is the kingdom's capital. As Clark and Waller (2007: 5) point out, commentators fall all too often into the error of making statements that purport to be about the UK, but are, in fact, only true of England. We did our best to avoid that error in the first edition of this book. This chapter takes things even further forward by examining systematically early years policy in Wales, Scotland and Northern Ireland.

Some independent states have federal constitutions; some are much more centralized, although with local administrations that will always have some measure of autonomy. The UK is set up rather differently 'neither unitary nor federal, but ... a union state' (Pilkington, 2002: 7). England, Wales, Scotland and Northern Ireland each have a different relationship to the kingdom as a whole, a relationship determined by different histories. (The Channel Islands and the Isle of Man have constitutional positions that are different again. However, initiatives there have had less impact on the rest of the kingdom and for this reason we have left consideration of their position on one side.)

The UK is not unique in having various kinds of devolution. In Spain the 'communities' that make up the state have different degrees of autonomy, with Catalonia and Euskadi (the Basque country) coming closest to complete home rule – and these arrangements were established in one brief period during the return to democracy in the late 1970s and early 1980s. The 'asymmetric' form of devolution in Spain has proved relatively stable and the same could prove to be true of the UK. However, differences in local powers can be seen as unfair and fuel debate as to whether there should be a more systematic approach (including devolution for England or for regions within England).

The support of young children has been one of the areas of policy most clearly under the control of the devolved governments in Wales, Scotland and Northern Ireland. It was also an area that had been comparatively neglected in these countries before devolution. One result of this has been that the devolved governments have often seen it as a sphere in which they could demonstrate their competence and progressive thinking. For example, in July 2001, when Northern Ireland began consultation on a strategy for children, Dermott Nesbitt, the Deputy First Minister, expressed the hope that the strategy would make his country a 'world leader' (*Nursery World*, 2001: 6).

The interest that many politicians in the three nations take in early years policy has been encouraged by lobbyists in England. It was already established practice there to compare the UK unfavourably with other countries, particularly with Spain, New Zealand, Denmark and the region of Reggio Emilia in Italy, all of which were said to provide models we should copy. Devolution has provided a new stick with which to beat those making policy for England. Thus Bruce (2001) spoke warmly of her experience of early years work in Scotland (Rawstrone, 2001) and Lindon (2005) praised the Scottish guidance on the birth-to-three curriculum, claiming that it was superior to the similar moves in England. It is significant that it was in 2001 and 2002 that *Nursery World* provided unusually detailed coverage of developments in the devolved countries, since this was the period when policy there (on standards in childminding and the role of the Children's Commissioner) was more in tune with the thinking of a majority of early years practitioners than was policy in England.

Given the way in which developments in the three countries have been used in debate, it is worth pointing out that England is not always bottom of the league in terms of what the early years profession views as best practice. The scale of provision has often been better in England. England took some steps to modify the artificial distinction in law and institutional arrangements between care and education before the other three nations. The NCH report *United for Children?* (2003) offers a more measured comparison of the four nations, although still critical of developments in England.

Comparing Wales, Scotland and Northern Ireland

The next three sections of this chapter provide some basic information on early years policy in Wales, Scotland and Northern Ireland. Each country is considered in relation to five issues:

▶ the history of its devolved powers

▶ the integration of services for young children

▶ the expansion of early years services since 1997

▶ quality, curriculum development and regulation

▶ comparison with other parts of the UK.

Wales

Devolution

The gradual conquest of Wales by England in the Middle Ages led to absorption into England under the Tudors. In the nineteenth century there was a systematic attempt to eliminate the Welsh language and children were punished for using it in school, even in the playground. It was not until 1907 that the first step was taken towards separate administration for Wales with the establishment of a Welsh Section in the Department of Education. In 1951 a Ministry of Welsh Affairs was set up under the Home Office (which then had a very wide remit). In 1957 responsibility for oversight of that ministry was transferred to Housing and Local Government. A Welsh Office was set up at Westminster in 1964. That body acquired responsibility for health in 1968 and for education in 1970. However, legislation continued for some time to be written for 'England and Wales' rather than for each country separately.

At the end of the 1970s there was a half-hearted and unsuccessful attempt by the Labour government to establish a form of devolved government for Wales. Devolution was one of the commitments of the Labour Party when it won the General Election of 1997. The first Government of Wales Act was passed in 1998 and the first elections for the Welsh Assembly were held in 1999. Tony Blair seems to have assumed that Wales would be content with a minimal level of autonomy and initially the posts of First Secretary of the Assembly and the Secretary of State for Wales were held by the same person. Rebellion in the Welsh Labour Party led to an end to this arrangement and later to the Government of Wales Act (2006), which gave the Assembly primary jurisdiction over all its own domestic affairs. Developments in early years are seen as key to overall education policy. In particular, they have been seen as crucial to the success of attempts to promote the Welsh language, now spoken by an increasing number of people, especially the young.

Integration

Across the UK there have been moves since 1997 to break down artificial divisions between care and education in services for very young children and to establish a more 'integrated' approach. Some have hoped that Children's Commissioners would have a key role to play in this process. Wales was the first country in the UK to show a strong interest in this idea, but the creation of a commissioner post was blocked by the Conservatives and, initially, by the 1997 Labour government. An inquiry into abuse in children's homes in Wales (Waterhouse, 2000) galvanized interest in the idea of a commissioner as well as in improvements in child protection. Legislation followed, creating for the first time anywhere in the UK a post of Children's Commissioner. This was also the first piece of legislation in the UK to make specific reference to the United Nations Convention on the Rights of the Child. Peter Clarke, the first Children's Commissioner for Wales, took up post in 2001.

The controversy over whether there should be a commissioner tended to overshadow progress on integration in other areas. By 2006 there was at least one Children's Centre in each of the 22 local authority areas in Wales and these were seen by many as being based on better models than the similar agencies in England (Seaton, 2006). As in the rest of the UK, integration was conducted on the basis of an assumption of lead responsibility by the education profession.

Expansion

Childcare was not well developed in Wales before devolution. As late as 1986 there was only one full day care setting throughout the country. The number of such settings in England would have been much lower then than it is now, but not as low as that. As recently as 2006 there was only one childcare place for every seven children under the age of eight in Wales. Reliance on informal care by grandparents and others remained a strong factor (Clark and Waller, 2007: 142). In 2001 the Assembly conducted a consultation of the public on its overall 'Plan for Wales' which dealt with priorities in childcare, education and health. The Assembly government was already committed to ensuring that early education was available to all children whose parents sought it and that out-of-school care was similarly available to all by 2010. Subsidized childcare is one of the key aspects of the Genesis Project (part funded by the European

Union) which was set up to reduce barriers faced by parents returning to work. A larger-scale investment began with the 'Flying Start' programme (2005–08) under which £46 million was spent on children and families in deprived areas on childcare and various forms of family support. As a result of these and other initiatives, there has been a significant increase in the number of places available (nearly 19,000 in the first five years of the Assembly's operation). As in other parts of the UK, promotion of childcare has been seen by the Labour Party as a means of encouraging parents back to work at least as much as it has been seen in terms of the needs of children. In this respect it is significant that the Childcare Working Group set up by the Assembly government in 2004 was chaired by the Minister for Economic Development and Transport.

Quality, curriculum development and regulation

Even before devolution there was a separate approach in Wales to quality and the curriculum, partly because of the increasing readiness of Westminster to allow some concessions to the Welsh language in the education system. This was strengthened by the decisions taken in 1996 on the Welsh equivalent of the framework for desirable learning outcomes in pre-school education. From the start the Welsh framework was seen as superior to the English one, with a stronger focus on the child as learner and an open-minded approach to the value of play. This has been a source of considerable pride in Wales. The powers of the Welsh Assembly include control over curriculum issues. In 2003 a new Foundation Phase was proposed and a revised version of that guidance was produced in January 2008. In comparison with the new Foundation Stage guidance that came into force in England in September 2008 and which makes only a slight dent in the barrier between pre-school and school education in the child's fifth year, the Welsh Foundation Phase will lead to the abolition of the current Key Stage 1 and is bound to impact significantly on Key Stage 2. It also continues the Welsh traditions of heavy emphasis on the role of play and of ascribing value to Welsh. (Among other things it identifies a seventh area of learning in addition to the six originally devised for England and Wales – one that focuses on cultural diversity, a development of the original focus on bilingualism). Moreover, the new phase was introduced with even greater care than its English equivalent, with a formal pilot in 41 settings monitored by a team led by Iram Siraj-Blatchford and Kathy Sylva. The final version was presented in October 2007. Full implementation will take place in 2011.

Related initiatives include:

▸ the pioneering role played by the Welsh Assembly government in the development of new approaches to the safeguarding of children, moves which pre-dated and influenced the 2004 Children Act

▶ the launch of a National Play Strategy in 2006

▶ changes in the system of initial teacher education and training

▶ a common inspection framework applying to all settings, introduced in 2008

▶ the *Good Practice Guidance for Out-of-Classroom Learning* issued by the Assembly government at the end of 2007.

Wales and the rest of the UK

Many of these developments have strong parallels with those in the rest of the UK. Wales has moved towards closer integration of services and seen childcare to a large extent in terms of getting parents off benefits and back to work. Part of the explanation for these similarities is that the Labour Party has been the dominant party in Wales as it has in the UK as a whole. However, there are some strong points of contrast, among them:

▶ the energy with which the Welsh Assembly has tackled this issue, typified in its determination to secure a Children's Commissioner

▶ the emphasis on play

▶ the more radical approach to the question of when formal schooling should begin

▶ the approach to cultural diversity that follows from the commitment to promoting the Welsh language.

There are, however, areas where Welsh and English policy are still very similar. For example, the Welsh Code of Practice for special needs is clearly based on the English one.

Scotland

Devolution

Unlike Wales, Scotland remained independent of England until the beginning of the eighteenth century. When the two countries were first united (in the early seventeenth century) it was on the basis of having the same monarch (James I and VI) rather than because Scotland had been conquered or absorbed in some way. Scotland had its own Parliament until 1707. Divisions between different parts of the country were at that time as important politically as any division between Scotland and England. After the unification of the two Parliaments differences remained in the legal and educational systems. A separate Scottish Office was established in Westminster as early as 1885.

When the Labour Party attempted to introduce devolution in Wales in 1979 a similar attempt was made for Scotland, one that was also unsuccessful. Margaret Thatcher was deeply opposed to devolution. However, once in power, Tony Blair moved rapidly to set up a new form of government for Scotland and in 1998 the Scotland Act laid the basis for a Scottish Parliament with its own Executive (later re-named the Scottish Government). The areas under the control of the Scottish Parliament include all those relevant to early years policy. Like Wales, Scotland continues to send MPs to the Westminster Parliament and the UK government retains control over significant areas of policy, including defence and foreign affairs. Initially at any rate, the Scottish Parliament had wider powers than the equivalent Assembly in Wales. Devolution (rather than full independence or full union with England) appears to have the support of a large section of the Scottish people (Bromley et al., 2006). In 2007 the Scottish National Party (SNP) emerged as the largest party in elections to the Scottish Government, although without an absolute majority. The SNP formed the new government, which included Scotland's first Minister for Children and Early Years – Adam Ingram – who spoke of his ambitions for young children. However, this was a matter of detail and emphasis rather than outright conflict between the parties. As the Chief Executive of the Scottish Out-of-School network said, 'all the major parties seem to agree on putting money into childcare' (Marcus, 2007: 5).

Integration

Scotland has pursued the concept of integrated services for young children with some eagerness and has won the admiration of many in England as a result. The first integrated service for young children in the UK was established in Strathclyde in the 1980s, well before local authorities in England were legally obliged to go in that direction in 2001 and ahead of those pioneering authorities in England that set up such services in the 1990s. In some respects integration has gone less far in Scotland than in England. For example, there are still separate systems for regulation and inspection of childcare and early education. Nevertheless, there have been significant moves towards integration, including:

▶ the New Community Schools programme launched in 1998

▶ the early establishment of a post of Children's Commissioner

▶ the policy document *For Scotland's Children* (Scottish Executive, 2001), which laid down an overall approach to integration

▶ the establishment of local Childcare Partnerships, similar to the EYDCPs in England, but held by some to have been more successful

▶ joint inspection of child protection services

▶ the development of a new BA degree for integrated services developed by a partnership of James Watt College and the University of Strathclyde

▶ the new framework for qualifications and professional development introduced by the Scottish Social Services Council in late 2007.

Expansion

In the period since devolution there has been significant expansion in early years services, particularly in after-school care and integrated pre-school centres. At times this has been seen as threatening maintained provision (partly because it has happened at a time of falling birth rates that already placed some maintained settings at risk). When it formed the new government in 2007 the SNP had a long-standing commitment to provide funding to support childcare and early education, and took a number of initiatives. These included the decision to provide £15 million to extend free pre-school education from 33 to 38 weeks as part of a set of major funding proposals for education as a whole, building on plans already formulated in 2006.

Quality, curriculum development and regulation

The system of education in Scotland has always differed from that in England in several respects. Neither the National Curriculum nor standard assessment tests (SATs) nor the literacy and numeracy hours were ever imposed north of the border. Devolution has encouraged further change. As in Wales, ideas on the earliest phase of the curriculum are integral to plans for schooling as a whole. Thus the work being conducted early in 2008 on curriculum guidance was concerned with the age range three to eighteen years rather than birth to five as in England. In 2007 the Scottish Social Services Council published new regulations on the qualifications of managers in all early years settings. In 2008 the Scottish Care Commission announced a number of changes in the inspection system, including a new grading system and a greater use of self-assessment in the inspection process. Scotland has also pioneered the further development of outdoor play. The first completely outdoor nursery in the UK was established in Fife and in early 2008 there were new funding initiatives to support outdoor play by the Scottish Government and by Aberdeenshire Council.

Scotland and the rest of the UK

The excellent work that has been done on some aspects of curriculum development in Scotland and the pioneering initiatives taken even before devolution on the integration of early years services have won praise in England for Scottish achievements. This may sometimes give a misleading impression of the contrast. The integration of inspection in the area of child protection can divert attention from the fact that Scotland still has systems for the regulation of early years childcare and education services that are separate in a way that they no longer are in England. The fact that the country is working towards a single set of curriculum guidance for ages three to eighteen can divert attention from the fact that the guidance for children under three remains quite separate. The electoral victory of the SNP in 2008 will certainly bring about some additional funding. Whether it brings about more significant reform is yet to be seen. The SNP government has already decided to postpone the roll-out of a funding programme designed to provide free nursery education for vulnerable children under two, which had been piloted in three local authorities.

Northern Ireland

Devolution

If there was violence in the history of England's relationships with Wales and Scotland, that fact was largely forgotten in modern times – at least in England. Both Scotland and Wales have political parties that are seeking full independence from the UK and the process of devolution has been marked by bitter argument. Nevertheless, devolution itself has been implemented with nothing much worse than the odd shouting match. The history of Northern Ireland is different. It has entailed not only wars in the distant past, but rebellion in the early twentieth century and armed conflict for much of the last part of that century. Previous forms of devolution have foundered on conflict within the province. Whereas the choice in Wales and Scotland has been between full union, full independence or a form of devolved government, the choices in Northern Ireland have been between full union with the UK, full union with the Irish Republic or a form of devolution that represents some kind of compromise between those two national identities.

It now seems that the re-established system of devolved government achieved in 2007 has a solid chance of continuing to make progress rather than of breaking down as other attempts have done, especially as it is based on agreement between the two bodies that had been seen as representing extremes of opinion – the Democratic Unionist Party (DUP) and Sinn Fein (the Irish nationalist party).

Well-deserved praise in both the Republic of Ireland and the USA has been heaped on Tony Blair and others who managed to broker this unexpected deal. However, mediators cannot magic agreement out of thin air. It seems likely that it was exhaustion after years of conflict, the economic prizes offered by peace, the increasing secularization of the Republic of Ireland that assuaged Protestant fears of the Catholic Church and the dawning realization on both sides in Northern Ireland that England and its politicians were relatively neutral on the future of the province rather than being committed to the union that, together, created the context in which real peace could be established. The DUP and Sinn Fein have shown themselves capable of working together on bread-and-butter social and economic issues, including early years policy. Sinn Fein, in particular, has a strong commitment to education – something it has in common with other forms of late nineteenth century republicanism, but which the party itself would relate to the illegal 'hedge schools' provided for the Catholic population during the long struggle for independence. A major feature of the new regime is increased cooperation with the Republic of Ireland, which has manifested itself in joint action to develop better child protection systems and the establishment of an all-Ireland service for children with autistic disorders.

Integration

There is still an institutional division in Northern Ireland between the care and education of young children, a division that may have been aggravated by the fact that social services in the province have institutional arrangements with many similarities to those in the Republic of Ireland while education has more in common with England. The division manifests itself largely in a separation of childcare for the under-threes and pre-school education for three- and four-year-olds. This is, of course, similar to the situation in Scotland. Just as in England some see a tension between the demands of the National Curriculum at Key Stage 1 and the implications of the curriculum guidance for the Foundation Stage, so in Northern Ireland there is seen to be a degree of tension between the demands of the revised National Curriculum (due to be fully implemented by 2010) and the play-based 'Enriched Curriculum' for younger children piloted in 120 schools across the province from 2001 to 2006 and now part of the new National Curriculum. Before the current agreement on devolution the Department of Education had attempted to protect pre-school settings by restricting the provision of reception class places, measures that came into effect in September 2007. (Again, there are parallels with Scotland.) Northern Ireland has also promoted a new integrated approach to children's services with the creation of posts of Children's Commissioner and, later, Children's Minister and greater cooperation between agencies at local level. In 2007 the Department for Education in Northern Ireland (DENI) assumed responsibility for the province's Sure Start programmes, the first stage in its acquisition of central responsibility for all children's services that was announced in 2006.

Expansion

Even before the general election of 1997 Northern Ireland had taken steps towards the promotion of early years services with the establishment of inter-agency Early Years Committees in each Health and Social Services area (as in the Republic of Ireland, Northern Ireland has a unified structure for the delivery of both health and social services through regional boards). After 1997 two reports were published from Westminster outlining plans for the development of early years learning and childcare services, plans similar to those being developed for England. By 2004 many of the targets set in those two reports had been met or surpassed.

Quality, curriculum development and regulation

The quality of staff involved in early years services has been a major issue and it is only in the recent past that cooperation with the Republic of Ireland and with the rest of the UK has led to the development of something like adequate vetting procedures. Criticisms of the over-formality of teaching in Year 1 of primary education suggest the need for further work on training and qualifications. However, considerable work has been undertaken on curriculum development. There has been a review of the Special Needs Code of Practice (largely borrowed from England). The EPPE project in England has been mirrored in a similar study in Northern Ireland (EPPNI) under the direction of Professor Edward Melhuish. Northern Ireland, often in close cooperation with agencies in the Republic of Ireland, is pioneering some interesting work in the field of special needs. One of the province's largely unnoticed achievements over the last 40 years has been the research work undertaken at the University of Ulster on cognitive development in the early years, especially where that is affected by visual and hearing impairments. Regulatory regimes have been less well developed in some respects than in England, but a new Education and Skills Authority was established in 2008 to bring together the work of several existing bodies and this should lead to improvements in this sphere. The authority is being asked to tackle not just the issue of inter-professional coordination, but the much more tricky issue of cooperation across the sectarian divide.

Northern Ireland and the rest of the UK

Wales and Scotland have both had significant contacts with regions in other countries that have achieved a significant measure of devolved power in recognition of their separate national identities. In particular, both the Scottish Labour Party and the SNP have had continuing contacts with the major parties in Catalonia in Spain where interesting initiatives in early years services have occurred. There have been similar moves on the part of the Labour Party in Wales and Plaid Cymru, both of which have been interested in the 'normalization' of the Catalan language and the implications for Welsh.

Northern Ireland is unique among the countries of the UK in having a special relationship (underpinned by a growing number of institutional arrangements) with a completely independent state, the Republic of Ireland. As fears among the Unionist/Protestant community about the implications of this contact slowly diminish, these contacts could begin to prove especially fruitful and introduce new elements into the internal debate in the UK on early years services.

Activity

Imagine a child born in the part of the UK that you know best in 2005. Define the child's social and economic situation in general terms. (Are his/her parents rich or poor or middle income? Does the family live in an urban or rural area? Are they part of the majority population or from a minority ethnic group? And so on.) Again, you should bear in mind the kind of situation with which you are most familiar.

▸ Describe the child's likely experiences of childcare and education services up to the age of seven.

▸ Do you think things would have been different if she had been born in similar social circumstances, but in another part of the UK?

Remember to go to the 'Useful Websites' page at the end of the book, where you will find the 4 Nations Child Policy Network website listed; this has information and links to websites relating to the individual countries that make up the UK.

The impact of devolution

This chapter has highlighted both similarities and differences between the countries comprising the UK and the ways in which they have influenced each other in the development of early years services.

At times there has been a kind of competition between them with lobbyists urging their own countries to emulate what they see as best practice in one or more of the other countries. Among the reasons have been

▸ genuine concern about the well-being of young children

▸ the fact that there was a lack of development before devolution, so that there was a lot of catching up to do

▶ the lead offered by the Blair government in London

▶ the new opportunities created by devolution.

However, it seems likely that a perfectly natural wish to do visibly better than England, the dominant partner in the union, comes into the equation.

The fact that contrasts are often made between what happens in Westminster and the initiatives taking place under devolved governments sometimes overshadows other and equally interesting comparisons. There are, for example, many similarities between Scotland and Northern Ireland and between those two countries and France, a country whose early years policy is rarely afforded consideration in the UK. Closer attention to comparisons between the countries with devolved powers, rather than between them and England, probably has some interesting lessons to reveal.

More attention might also be paid to issues of national identity and culture. The place of Welsh in the education system has been a very live issue in Wales. However, overall there is very little evidence to suggest that Wales, Scotland and Northern Ireland are developing specifically 'national' solutions to the needs of young children. This might have been expected. In Spain the significant developments in education and social welfare policies that have taken place in Catalonia and Euskadi have been built on what has been seen as the best professional practice from abroad rather than on aspects of national identity. Indeed, some in the UK have argued strongly that the needs of children are universal and that, therefore, there should be very few differences, if any, between policies in different parts of the UK (for example, Kullas, 2000). This is an issue that could become increasingly contentious not just in the context of devolution, but in the context of allegations that 'multiculturalism' has failed.

Point for reflection 〰️

There are some who argue that all parts of the UK should have essentially the same standards in early years services because the needs of young children remain essentially the same wherever they are.

Others argue that different developments in different parts of the UK are helpful because:

▶ they facilitate experimentation

▶ they can reflect differences in national identity

▶ they can reflect different demands from the public in different places.

Outline what you think are the main arguments that can be made for or against the differences in policy to which devolution has led.

Summary ☐

This chapter has shown how:

▶ there are a number of differences between early years policies in the four major parts of the UK

▶ devolution has created new opportunities to develop early childcare and education

▶ devolution has also, to some extent, created competition in a way that has probably helped to speed up developments in this sphere.

Further reading 📖

Welsh, F. (2002) *The Four Nations: A History of the UK*, London: HarperCollins. Offers a useful introduction to the broad historical context.

Pilkington, C. (2002) *Devolution in Britain Today*, Manchester; Manchester University Press. Good on the early development of devolved powers.

Clark, M. and Waller, T. (eds) (2007) *Early Childhood Education and Care*, London: Sage Publications. Offers an excellent description of early years policy in each of the four major parts of the UK (and in the Republic of Ireland). It provides much greater detail than has been possible in this chapter and has case studies that help the reader understand the impact of policy on individual children.

The Impact of Policy

Chapter 4 provided an overview of how policy is devised and clearly highlighted how the raft of policies within early years has led to a significant expansion of service provision. On one level this can be welcomed, as it would seem likely that this would lead to improvements for children and families. Nonetheless, it is necessary to explore the likely impact of the diverse policies on different stakeholders.

This chapter:

▶ explores how policy developments impact on three key groups – practitioners, children and parents

▶ aims to show how policy can offer potential benefits for one or more of the groups but at the same time may also create tensions

Since 1997 there have been some major shifts in early years policy. In many respects, as discussed in earlier chapters, the National Childcare Strategy provided an impetus that has led to significant changes in early years services, and the Children's Plan suggests this will continue. Over the past years the expectations from government, local authorities, other services and parents in regard to early years services have increased and there has been a massive increase in provision, including part-time funded places for three-year-olds (DCSF, 2007a). There is a much greater focus on having practitioners with professional qualifications, a more rigorous inspection process to drive up quality throughout the sector and an expectation that future service provision will work in partnership not only with parents but also with a range of other services drawn from health and social care as well as education. Overall, these changes seem positive, but to understand the impact on practitioners, children and parents requires more in-depth consideration.

Practitioners

The early years workforce is diverse, in terms of the qualifications and experience it holds. However, there are some areas where this diversity is not evident, for example age, where more than a third of the workforce is below the age of 25. It is also significant that approximately 99 per cent are women, there are few practitioners from ethnic minorities, few with disabilities and the majority of practitioners hold a qualification at or below Level 3 (for example, CACHE Diploma, BTEC National Diploma). Another significant difference is that over half of early years practitioners work in the profit sector, compared with less than 10 per cent of teachers (Office for National Statistics, 2003). One reason for these differences, which has been discussed in previous chapters, is the division of responsibility between care and education. The term 'early years care and education' is often now used, with the aim of breaking down artificial barriers between care and education as the boundaries between each are generally unclear and young children need both, not one or the other. This is also reflected in local authorities with the merger of child social services and education departments and the creation of Director of Children's Services posts to lead the formed departments. Nonetheless, even when account is taken of recent developments, care has often been seen as inferior to education and this is reflected in the qualification level, perception, training opportunities and salary level of practitioners: with those practitioners within the early years sector who are not qualified teachers being seen with less regard than those with qualified teacher status. In terms of conditions of employment as well as low pay, this often entails working longer hours and absence of other benefits such as sick pay and time/funding for professional development (Osgood, 2004).

When this is seen in the context of government plans for workforce expansion and professionalization this raises fundamental questions. The ten-year strategy released by the government, which sets out its plans for early years services, identifies the importance of the early years workforce in achieving the ambitious strategies on the plan (HM Treasury et al., 2004). Many of these points were reiterated in the recently published Children's Plan, which clearly emphasizes the importance of workforce development in creating a world-class early years care and education system (DCSF, 2007a). The basis of this is the simple realization, but it is important to acknowledge that the quality of early years settings is clearly integrated with the quality of practitioners. The EPPE project (Sylva et al., 2004), which has tracked outcomes for over 3,000 children who have experienced various types of day care (for example, LEA-run nurseries, community playgroups and integrated centres), found that:

▸ the higher the qualification level of practitioners, particularly the leaders in each setting, the better the quality of the setting and the outcomes for children

▸ settings led by graduates were particularly effective and this has to be seen in the light of the current situation where qualification levels are low

▸ access to training was variable in a significant number of settings, particularly those in the profit sector where there is extremely high turnover of staff, which creates inconsistency and difficulties in sustaining a work-force that is able to continue their professional development over time.

Based on government plans for child and family services this presents significant challenges in achieving many of the ambitious targets in two main areas: leadership of early years settings and creating a sustainable workforce.

Leadership in the early years workforce has not received the same level of attention as in other sectors of education, particularly schools. One difficulty for the early years sector is the fragmented range of services that make up provision. This ranges from multiple-site private nursery chains to integrated centres that provide a range of health, social and educational services to community-run playgroups (which in some areas, such as rural areas, may be the only provision available). In expanding services, the Labour government, in its attempt to keep a central hold on developments, has taken a managerialist approach to funding and provision, which has led to a range of demands on setting leaders, including increased administration, a range of targets to achieve and complicated requirements to attract and maintain funding (Osgood, 2004). This raises issues about the balance between the complexity of centrally imposed management requirements and the demands on each type of provider. For example, a large Children's Centre may be able to respond to a broader range of requirements than a childminder working independently and offering provision for a group of children at varied times during the week. This is not meant to suggest that large-scale private provision is better or more effective. In fact some of the most successful provision, designated as Early Excellence Centres, started as locally based voluntary sector provision (Osgood, 2004). Within these settings there was an emphasis on collaborative and cooperative working at the same time as responding to the government's agenda of reducing social exclusion. For policy development and implementation this emphasizes the need to consider further developments carefully and ensure that account is taken of the need to develop collaborative practice, rather than simply assume that policy alone can achieve this.

As part of its ten-year strategy for childcare, the government has signalled a commitment to increase the number of Children's Centres to 3,500 by 2010 (by the end of 2007 there were over 1,500 centres). These centres provide an integrated range of services to meet the social, health and educational requirements of children and families. The diverse range of services that children's services will provide will require leadership from appropriately qualified and skilled practitioners if the full potential of the policy for integrated services is to be realized. In response to this the government, for the first time, has acknowledged the need for a range of skilled practitioners, including graduates in early years (HM Treasury et al., 2004). This move is welcome as there is a large body of evidence that shows the need for effective leadership in education, although less on leadership in early years (Muijs et al., 2004). Kagan and Hallmark (2001) argue that leadership in early years encompasses a number of roles:

- ▸ administrative skills

- ▸ pedagogical leadership

- ▸ an ability to lead community services and initiatives

- ▸ the ability to act as an advocate for groups and show political awareness.

This highlights the need for effective education up to degree level and effective leadership training. Other groups, such as universities providing Early Childhood Studies courses, children's organizations and sectors of the academic community have argued the need for this for several years. A positive development has been the announcement of the Graduate Leadership Fund (DCSF, 2008). The fund, which replaces the transformation fund, is allocated to local authorities and the CWDC and aims to raise standards and enhance quality through the provision of graduates in settings. The fund is intended to provide scope to attract new graduates into the sector and provide resources to enable practitioners already within the sector to train to graduate level. A welcome development with this fund is that there is a commitment to provide resources through this channel until at least 2015, which enables local authorities and early years settings to plan on a more long-term basis rather than from year to year. In addition, the fund is primarily focused on the private, voluntary and independent (PVI) sector where only 3 per cent of the workforce, compared with over 40 per cent in the maintained sector, are graduates. The two main graduate opportunities available within the sector are through the Early Years Professional Status (EYPS) or National Professional Qualification in Integrated Centre Leadership (NPQICL). These routes offer either graduate or postgraduate training for practitioners. With EYPS, which the CWDC see as having equivalency to qualified teacher status, practitioners are trained to take a lead role in planning and delivering the curriculum. With NPQICL, which is similar in nature to the National Professional Qualification for Headship (NPQH), holders generally take a management and leadership role. There is an expectation that Children's Centres managers will attain this qualification and it has relevance across education, health and social care (National College for School Leadership, 2008).

In addition to having good leaders in the early years sector, to achieve the ambitious expansion plans and targets set in policy documents a systematic overhaul of the early years workforce will be needed. As well as the importance of the early years workforce in terms of sustainability, there is a clear link between the skill level of the workforce and quality (DCSF, 2007a; HM Treasury et al., 2004). At present, early years practitioners cover a continuum of experience and qualifications. This ranges from little past experience and no formal qualifications to Level 3 qualifications, such as CACHE diplomas or BTEC Early Years qualifica-

tions, to degrees, such as Early Childhood Studies or qualified te
those with qualified teacher status, who usually work in scho
either within maintained nurseries, reception classes or found
terms and conditions of service are set within national agreeme
by these. But, as stated earlier, for the majority of practitioners
the level of reward, working conditions and opportunities for
progression do not match those of practitioners with qualified teacher status
the majority are not covered by national agreements on pay and conditions. To
address this situation there will need to be a radical rethink of how policy can
take account of and be applied to the fragmented range of early years services.
This will need to explore how best to support and develop their workforce to
ensure that early years care and education services are of high quality, sustainable and take account of the expectations of children and parents. An Integrated
Qualifications Framework (IQF), which is expected to be fully developed in 2010,
is being developed by the Children's Workforce Network (CWN, 2008). Although
progress has been slow, it is the first real attempt to develop a coherent and integrated approach to progression and continuing professional development for
practitioners. From 2010, all qualifications held by practitioners within the early
years sector will be part of the framework and this should assist practitioners,
who cross a number of traditional professional boundaries, to continue to
progress within the early years sector by building on qualifications and experience gained in other related and relevant fields.

In 2004 a National Audit Office report of early years services identified three
key issues to creating sustainable provision: lack of premises, lack of trained
workforce and withdrawal of start-up funding (NAO, 2004). The report drew
attention to the importance of not only creating places, but of sustaining them
also. One of the greatest challenges in terms of sustainability could arguably
be ensuring an adequate supply of appropriately qualified practitioners for
expanding early years services and ensuring there are processes in place that
value and reward these people once they are in post.

Activity

Think about each of the following and if possible talk to practitioners with
different experiences to gain their perspective:

▸ What level of qualification should early years practitioners have?
   Explain why you think this.

▸ Is there a need for some/all practitioners within early years to be educated to degree level? Explain why you think this.

▸ What may be the barriers to attracting people to work in early years
   services?

continued

> ▶ What measures are needed to keep practitioners within early years services?
>
> ▶ Is there a clear career pathway for practitioners in early years? If not, what would need to be done to establish one?

When thinking about each of these points an important consideration should be the diversity of early years services. Unlike schools, which generally have a similar pattern of organization (but do not necessarily offer the same experiences for children), early years services span a range of providers. For example, there are childminders who may work predominantly in isolation in local communities; private organizations with multiple sites; Children's Centres, which may be voluntary or local authority operated and provide a diverse array of educational, social and health support services. What is clear from an accumulating body of evidence is that the higher the overall qualification of practitioners the greater the quality of early years care and education they offer (DCSF, 2007a; Sylva et al., 2004). Arguably the workforce issue and, up to a point, the issue of providing more consistent frameworks for developing practitioners has been tackled but several years on there remains a sustainability issue and in many respects the need to address this is even more pressing, based on the expectations set out in the Childcare Act (2006).

However, to achieve the ambitious plans recently outlined, future policy will require far more than simply putting graduates into the workplace. Moss (2004) draws attention to Target 26 set by the European Commission Childcare Network in 1995 which set the ambitious aim, for the UK at least, of ensuring that a minimum of 60 per cent of practitioners working with children have completed at least three years of post-18 training (for example, degree level) and that the remainder of staff without this should have access to it either at training institutions or through continuous professional development. Even so, increased training levels alone are not enough. To value practitioners, with increased levels of training, there also needs to be a rethink of salary levels, clearer progression routes for practitioners and a career framework that makes this possible (HM Treasury et al., 2004) and over the past years there has been little progress in these areas. The government outlined a commitment to addressing these issues, but it remains to be seen how great an impact this will have on creating a sustainable workforce (Hill, 2005). The Children's Workforce Development Council is beginning to assist in the creation of a strong workforce that is able effectively to meet the needs of children and young people and certainly has good intentions but it remains to be seen whether the ambitious targets set for 2015 are achieved (DCSF, 2008b).

Since the election of the Labour government in 1997, there has been an increased emphasis on providing integrated early years services, but the current set-up of services in many ways makes this difficult to achieve. Evidence of this can be provided by exploring two different examples. For a number of years there has been a decline in the number of registered childminders. To provide integrated services it is necessary for practitioners to work in partnership with a range of stakeholders. For childminders this can involve working with the local authority, the NCMA, the Children's Information Service (CIS) and parents. Although this may seem unproblematic, when it is considered alongside other aspects of their role, such as meeting the expectations of the Early Years Foundation Stage (DfES, 2007a), marketing their service, attending training and managing finances, this shows the complex nature of the role and potentially highlights how the mismatch between expectations and reward has led to significant reductions in numbers. In response to this a number of pilot projects have been established where coordinators have been appointed within local authorities to set up teams of support childminders. The role of the support childminders is to work with a small group of new childminders and offer them guidance and advice on different aspects of the role over the first year. Initial evaluation from the projects has been positive and has found that, with the support, many new childminders who have considered stopping had continued because of the scheme (NCMA, 2005). This is a clear example of how having appropriate support processes in place can have a positive impact on sustaining new provision and is an area often ignored by policy. However, over the past two years there has been an almost 10 per cent decrease in the number of childminders (Ofsted, 2006c) and as expectations increase, which is likely to be the case with the new curriculum, this may be exacerbated and this could have a negative impact on provision and parental choice.

Another example of the challenge of offering integrated services utilizing the skills of early years teachers is evidence from Sure Start schemes. Hastings (2004) undertook a telephone survey of 260 local programmes and found that only 12 per cent employed teachers in various roles, such as a community teacher or a pre-school teacher for children with special educational needs or English as an additional language. It was also found that it was more common for teachers to be employed on programmes managed by community or voluntary organizations rather than education authorities. But perhaps of greater significance were the issues identified around the reasons for deciding to employ teachers. There was found to be an association between employing teachers and promoting inclusion within schools. Other schemes, for example those where the lead agency was health related, did not see the relevance of employing teachers. Where schemes did employ teachers, they generally saw the benefit of having them (Hastings, 2004), but this suggests that the vast majority did not see the benefit of having teachers employed as part of the scheme. This is concerning for a number of reasons. As part of the public sector agreements linked to Sure Start, Objective 3 sets out an expectation on all schemes to improve children's ability to learn. Another expectation on all schemes is to take into account and promote the emotional and social well-being of children and families, which is now a central part of the EYFS. It is difficult and perhaps inappropriate to conclude from one telephone survey that teachers lack the skills needed to contribute to the work of SureStart Children's Centres, but there is clearly a need for well-qualified and experienced practitioners to take on demanding roles and if teachers are not able to do this it raises questions about who can.

With the change in service organization and integration it seems an ideal time to consider the roles of those who work within early years services. Questions exist about whether the current division of roles is appropriate to meet the demands that current and planned early years policies will place on providers and practitioners. Again the government acknowledged this in its ten-year childcare strategy by stating that a new profession, combining learning and care, is needed that will exist alongside teachers (HM Treasury et al., 2004). Moss (2004) draws attention to the need for such a role, often described as a pedagogue and similar to that seen in many European countries. The role of a pedagogue needs to be seen as different to that of a teacher and to have its own clear identity. Pedagogues will take a holistic approach to each child and family member and encompass a number of skills that will enable them to take account of the individual social, emotional and cultural identity of each person they work with. Similarities are likely to exist in terms of the training they receive, as they will be educated to degree level. Graduates from Early Childhood Studies degrees have followed courses focusing on the holistic needs of children and families, but in employment these skills are often not fully utilized, which is partly attributable to the lack of appropriate professional roles. In a number of European countries a pedagogue role exists, which encompasses supporting children's education and care and it spans health, social care and educational contexts (Fitzgerald and Kay, 2008). The Early Years Professional role covers aspects of this position but it is heavily focused on leading the curriculum in early years settings, and in the move to multi-agency working it may not help to achieve this. Anning (2004) refers to the need to develop 'a community of practice' within early years where knowledge is used in action and developed in ways acceptable to the community. This raises issues for integration and emphasizes the need for practitioners with a high level of skills in different aspects of early years care and education as well as education, and could be seen as further support for the role of pedagogues who are able to use their skills and knowledge to engage and make decisions to benefit children and families without over-dominance from the managerialist style that is often indirectly enforced through current arrangements and funding from the DCFS.

Children

The significant expansion of early years services now means that there are large numbers of children who experience some type of early years care and education. This may be in the form of one to two sessions per week in a pre-school setting, to five funded sessions in a nursery, or a mixture of provision from different providers on a full-time basis. When considering the impact of the many policy changes, it is important that the implications for children are considered. For example:

▸ Is increased provision appropriate for all children?

▸ Is the curriculum offered appropriate to the needs of children?

▸ Do practitioners have the necessary qualifications, experience and access to training?

▸ Is there support in place to meet the diverse developmental needs of each child?

When considering these issues, it is unlikely that there will be a simple yes or no answer. It is also important to understand that policy alone cannot be blamed for failures or praised for success. To make an evaluation of the provision for children it is necessary to evaluate if policies have laid the basis for high-quality and appropriate provision.

For children one of the most significant changes in early years care and education has been the introduction of a unified statutory curriculum (EYFS), which built on *Birth to Three Matters* (Sure Start Unit, 2002) for children aged from birth to three and the *Curriculum Guidance for the Foundation Stage* (QCA/DfEE, 2000). One positive impact of this has been that the provision for children in reception classes, which often lagged behind many maintained nurseries in terms of activities and facilities, has received much greater attention. This has included the appointment of Foundation Stage coordinators who are often members of school senior management teams, access to additional training for teachers in appropriate pedagogy for early years, a greater focus on outdoor play and more flexible and child-directed activities. But there are still concerns with provision in the Foundation Stage, particularly in some reception classes. For example, the qualifications of many practitioners may not be specific to early years, there are often low levels of support staff and some schools with mixed Foundation and Key Stage 1 classes (Aubrey, 2004), which can lead to an inappropriate curriculum for young children. A number of settings also have very limited outdoor space that children are able to access freely. It could be argued that many of these concerns cannot be attributed to policy failings, but new policy has the potential to address them.

Point for reflection 〰️

Think about the issues above and any other possible concerns that you have seen or discussed relating to foundation provision and jot them down.

▸ Which can be linked to potential policy shortfalls and which may be linked to other reasons?

▸ Are there any that have multiple causes or are difficult to place in one list or the other?

In terms of structural issues, such as the building or outdoor space (an area identified as in need of development in the Children's Plan), it can be argued that new policy developments which focus on appropriate pedagogy for early years cannot be linked with inopportune building design. With other issues, such as practitioner qualifications and training, it is more difficult to separate them. In many respects introducing a curriculum appropriate to the needs of young children is a positive step, but it would not be difficult to envisage that practitioners would be likely to need significant support and training to implement this policy to its full positive effect. The decision to have a separate curriculum for children from birth to five+ and then in Key Stage 1, could also be seen as continuing with poor policy, as it does nothing to reduce the issue of fragmentation in early years care and education provision and the start of formal schooling for younger children nor does it introduce a coordinated approach to learning. This also links to the current policy on school starting age that many criticize as too young and inappropriate for children (Dowling, 1999; Sharp, 2003). The provision of curriculum documents alone is also not the complete solution as there are still clear requirements on practitioners to promote and sustain interactions between children and ensure that activities provided are appropriately matched to children's levels of development (Siraj-Blatchford and Sylva, 2004; Siraj-Blatchford et al., 2008).

Since the National Curriculum was introduced there has been increasing criticism of the impact it has had on reducing the place of creativity within education. This was particularly acute for children in Key Stage 1 and reception classes, where the didactic approach of the Numeracy and Literacy Strategies was (and still is for children in Key Stage 1) experienced on a daily basis. In comparison, the child-centred pedagogical approach advocated in the Foundation Stage curriculum guidance was welcomed as a positive step forward and was seen as more likely to lead to child-initiated activities, sustained and extended by interaction between practitioners and children, and this positive step has been further developed in the new EYFS curriculum. The provision of the new document alone will not guarantee this, but the approach advocated throughout it (for example, giving children time to explore, gain understanding, problem-solve and make discoveries) is clearly in line with effective early years practice. But this is not meant to suggest that direct teaching is wrong. As Siraj-Blatchford and Sylva (2004: 726) highlight, 'Direct instruction is not harmful; it is the balance that is important', which again highlights the need for skilled practitioners. Interestingly, though, the move to embedding creativity as a key component of early years education took many years. Plowden (DES, 1967) highlighted the need for appropriate early years provision but in terms of acquiring knowledge and skills, whereas the Rumbold Report (DES, 1990) emphasized the need for a creative approach to ensure a greater coherence between education and care and to provide effectively for all aspects of children's development. It is only several years later, though, that this has been partially realized for children up to the age of five.

Another important consideration for children is whether there is a holistic policy approach to meet the emotional, social, health and physical aspects of development as well as the educational aspects. Kurtz (2003) identifies a wide-reaching policy approach to promote the health and well-being of children, not least through the Sure Start initiative, which places health at the centre of its agenda through the aim to tackle and reduce the impact of poverty and the links this has with low educational standards (Glass, 2001). Since 2000 there have been reductions in poverty rates, infant/child mortality and accidental injury, which suggests a successful policy agenda, as discussed further in Chapter 7. However, recent debates have highlighted how different interpretations from the same data can be made based on the definition of poverty used (Lister, 2004). In terms of absolute poverty (when a family lacks enough money to meet basic needs) progress has been made, but in terms of relative poverty (when a family lacks resources to have a good diet, participate in society and have access to amenities that are seen as customary in society) progress is more debatable. This is significant though as the central aim of the Sure Start unit is to promote inclusion and participation of disenfranchised families. The introduction of the National Service Framework for Children, Young People and Maternity Services, which sets ambitious health and treatment targets for all children, also confirms that there is a wide-ranging policy agenda to support all aspects of children's development (Department of Health/DfES, 2004). If the National Service Framework is to achieve the ambitious targets set for all children, a clear challenge will be to find ways to implement the policy across boundaries between networks of public, private and voluntary service providers (Masterson et al., 2004). It still remains to be seen whether the challenges this presents can be overcome.

Parents

The issue of partnership between providers and parents has become more significant over the past years and there is now a clear expectation, and rightly so, that providers need to work in a way that acknowledges the contribution parents make and values and respects their opinions. But the issue of partnership is often misunderstood and the term may be bandied about without full acknowledgement of the needs of parents (Jones, 2004). As the complexity of early years services has increased this has raised a number of issues for parents. To work effectively with parents requires policies that are joined up and responsive, which cannot be achieved through the provision of services alone. Services need to be available at times when parents require them, and must be accessible, affordable and integrated to provide consistency.

There are a variety of ways that practitioners can work in partnership with parents. Epstein and Saunders (2002) describe a continuum of partnership models that can be used by early years care and education settings but which also provides a basis for other services, to assess their level of partnership working with parents:

▸ *Protective model.* This operates along the lines of a business and requires parents to delegate responsibility for education to the setting as the aims of home and the setting and the roles of practitioners and parents are different.

▸ *School-to-home transmission model.* This model recognizes the importance of the family but only places an emphasis on one-directional communication – from the setting to the home – and assumes a level of parental agreement with decisions taken by the setting. In this model there is likely to be little sharing of ideas between the setting and community.

▸ *Curriculum enrichment model.* This model recognizes the benefits of collaborative learning between practitioners, parents and children, and integrates knowledge from families and the community into the curriculum and learning. There is a focus on the curriculum as this is seen as an important vehicle for impacting on learning

▸ *Partnership model.* This model is built on long-term commitment, mutual respect and widespread involvement of families and practitioners at different levels, such as joint planning and shared decision-making. It reflects the fact the children are embedded in and influenced by the home, the setting and the community.

Activity

Think about each stage of the model and settings that you have worked in or been on placement at.

▸ What examples have you seen of partnership working and which stage of the model would you place them at?

▸ Have you seen any particularly effective or poor examples of partnership working? What was it that made them effective or poor?

continued

> ▸ Think about one aspect of partnership working with parents (you could base this on something you have seen in practice) and write a brief outline of it.
>
> ▸ Identify where on the model you would place the setting.
>
> ▸ Draw up an action plan to work out how you would develop partnership working to the next stage of the partnership model. Compare the strategies you have identified with a partner.

The introduction of policies can lay the basis for partnership working with parents (and between professionals), but policy alone cannot ensure that this will be achieved. To achieve high levels of partnership working requires practitioners and families to work together in an open and respectful way. This requires practitioners to communicate effectively with families and each other, which can be challenging, particularly when services are delivered by a number of agencies. In this respect the challenges ahead for practitioners from different disciplines to work effectively with parents are significant.

Availability and accessibility of services is another key issue for parents. There is clearly a body of data to show there have been significant increases in early years provision, but it cannot be taken for granted that this equates with good levels of availability and accessibility for all children and families. To think about this more analytically, a number of questions have to be considered:

▸ Are services available equally in all areas (for example, urban and rural areas)?

▸ Are services affordable for all families?

▸ Are services available when families require them?

▸ If children attend more than one setting, are the different providers coordinated to ensure smooth transitions between them?

▸ Are there adequate transport facilities available for families to access the different providers they may need?

▸ Is the full range of services required by families provided in the same location?

Families living in rural areas often still face significant challenges in accessing appropriate and affordable services. This may be because there is simply a shortage of provision or what is provided is either not able to offer early years care and education for the required amount of time or not at affordable rates, but this is not confined to rural areas alone. The government has acknowledged this and has expressed a commitment to enhance the level of wrap-around provision to assist parents by providing integrated provision (DCSF, 2007a). A clear challenge in achieving this aim, though, will be moving the policy on extended school provision and increasing the number of childminders into practice. With regard to childminders, this is concerning because, as noted earlier, numbers are in decline. Another challenge faced by parents is organizing the daily family routine around early years care and education provision, and this becomes particularly challenging when there are children of different ages within the family (especially if there is a child below statutory school age and a child above). To access the different range of providers and fit this in with work and other family commitments can involve the family in negotiating complex plans, making numerous journeys and still often having to rely on informal care networks throughout the week (Skinner, 2003).

In terms of accessibility there has been success in government policy in attracting parents to services that previously may not have been affordable. The Neighbourhood Nurseries Initiative, which aimed to expand childcare provision in the 20 per cent most disadvantaged wards in England by providing start-up funding to encourage and support new provision, has been partially successful. Bell and La Valle (2005) found that:

▶ two-thirds of families using Neighbourhood Nursery provision had not previously used childcare facilities

▶ the provision was used by over half of parents in the early morning and late afternoon

▶ the level of satisfaction with the provision was generally high and that almost a fifth of parents had been able to enter work since accessing the nursery.

But further consideration is needed. Concerns have been raised about the sustainability of some Neighbourhood Nurseries Initiative provision and whether the service will remain viable as the initial support funding that the settings attract starts to reduce. The expectation is that as services grow in popularity, they will attract other sources of funding and increase the number of families using the setting and become self-sufficient. It is also necessary though to consider the location of these settings. They are located in areas where there are likely to be high rates of unemployment, the average wage for the locality may be low and the range of employment and training opportunities may be limited. Another issue is the implicit assumption that the aim of increased service provision is primarily to enable parents to enter the employment market. Another factor that can impact on participation in service provision is the attitude of current users. The aim of many children's centres is to attract 'hard to reach' families, but practitioners need to be aware of how the attitude of current users may impact on potential new users so that cliques do not stop potential new users feeling excluded. This can be a particular concern if a setting is located in a catchment area that draws families from varied socio-economic backgrounds (Sheppard et al., 2008). The Family Parenting Institute argue that there is a need for an overarching family policy to include often excluded groups from services, for example children with disabilities or parents with mental health problems. The number of policies that impact on families is vast and they generally develop in a piecemeal way across many government departments, and each needs to be 'family proofed'. A particular issue that still requires much more detailed attention is the level of support that is provided to families in the first 12 months after the birth of a child (Family Parenting Institute, 2005). There have been limited advances in this area with the introduction of the Parenting Fund, which has provided two rounds of funding for promoting good practice for family and parent support services (Family Parenting Institute, 2008). To address this a much more sustained effort will need to be made to support all parents, as well as targeting those in disadvantaged areas, if the outcomes for all children are to be raised.

The government agenda of reducing disadvantage and social exclusion is often tied to the success of policies that provide childcare places and enable parents, who previously were not employed, to return to work. This may be one method of judging the successfulness of policy developments, but other issues need to be considered for parents. The issue of work–life balance has developed momentum over recent years and is particularly significant to families with young children (DTI, 2004). In response to this the government announced improvements to the length of maternity and adoption leave and financial benefits to 39 weeks, with an eventual aim of raising these periods to 52 weeks (DTI, 2005). There have also been positive moves towards allowing parents of young children to ask their employers to consider adopting a flexible approach to working hours and the introduction, albeit minimal, of paid paternity leave. These issues highlight the need for policies to address a range of issues and to be focused on more than simply moving parents back into the employment market. The emphasis placed on the move from welfare to work by government is to some degree understandable as there is a correlation between being employed, the number of adults in a family and levels of poverty. Caution is still needed if new issues, such as reliance on a variety of providers for childcare and increased family stress levels, are not addressed in new developments. There is little point in formulating policies that move parents into work and simply replace one set of difficulties with another. To avoid this policy-makers need to see the holistic needs of families and ensure that policies are able to respond effectively to the diverse needs of each family.

Activity

You have been asked to write a short evaluative account of the impact of the Early Years Foundation Stage Curriculum as part of a review of early years provision for the CWDC. The account will be read by a range of providers, government departments and parents.

When planning your account it would be useful to think about the impact in terms of practitioners, children and parents. This will help to ensure that the response takes account of the impact on the key stakeholders and is more likely to identify the benefits and any difficulties from the curriculum. An important aspect of any written response to this type of activity is to support all claims with relevant evidence. This could come from a range of sources, including other reports, policy documents, academic papers, research studies and other relevant texts, for example, books on child development.

Your response is likely to have included a range of positive impacts and some drawbacks. There is a broad range of information that you could have drawn on. You may also have identified other relevant stakeholders that you feel should be considered. For example, the practitioner group could include people with very varied experiences. It may include individual practitioners who work in a large voluntary setting, an individual childminder or an owner/manager of a private nursery. This diversity within the initial groups may seem challenging. However, considering the perspective of a range of interested stakeholders and responding to this, particularly where it is supported by evidence, will include the quality and level of analysis within your response. The points below summarize some of the issues you may have considered for each group:

Practitioners

▶ The commitment to have at least one graduate in every setting, to deliver the curriculum, is likely to offer significant opportunities for practitioners to engage in continuing professional development.

▶ The curriculum draws together and builds on information from a range of sources (for example, national day-care standards for under eights, *Birth to Three Matters*, *Curriculum Guidance for the Foundation Stage*, primary strategies) and it may lead to a more coherent and less bureaucratic burden for practitioners.

▶ It places the role of practitioners in supporting children's development and welfare as central and this could help to professionalize the workforce.

▶ The demands of the curriculum will have different impacts. For example, for childminders it could add significantly to what is expected of them and they may not have access to appropriate support and training, or the resource implications of gaining this could be prohibitive.

▶ Linked to previous points the increased expectations and development opportunities need to be formally recognized and a career structure is likely to aid progression and retention of practitioners (to achieve the stated government aim of having a world-class workforce).

▶ It could aid inter-agency working, as all registered practitioners and settings will be working to the same unified and coherent curriculum.

Children

▶ Coordinated and joined up curriculum.

▶ Play-based curriculum, which is appropriate to supporting children's development.

▶ Holistic approach, which places equal value on social, emotional, physical and cognitive development.

▶ Takes careful account of children's welfare needs.

▶ Emphasizes that children develop at different rates and this is part of expected development.

▶ It provides a consistent approach across all settings, which will be particularly beneficial for children attending more than one setting.

▶ It promotes equality for all children and recognition of diversity.

▶ It views all children, from birth, as competent learners and sees them as capable.

▶ Children are encouraged to participate in their own learning, which is in line with the principles of the UNCRC.

▶ The appropriate approach to learning advocated by the curriculum is a stark contrast to the Key Stage 1 curriculum and children may find the transition point difficult.

Parents

▶ Sees parents at the heart of supporting their child's learning and development.

▶ Sets out clearly what parents can expect from early years care and education providers.

▶ For young children, particularly if parents are not familiar with early years care and education, the approach may seem very formal.

▸ The documented approach to early years care and education may be interpreted by parents as being superior to the care they, or family members, provide.

▸ It lays the foundation for inclusion of all children.

Your response to this activity may also include points which, although not directly related to the introduction of the statutory curriculum, are closely interlinked with it. This highlights both the challenges and fascination of gaining a clear insight into how policy has a widespread impact on practice and all those linked with it. What we hope is clear is that it is not possible to have a full understanding of how practice impacts on all stakeholders without at least some understanding of the policy that has led to current provision.

Summary

▸ This chapter has explored the impact of policy on different stakeholders by examining each group in turn, but in many respects this divide is artificial.

▸ The purpose of this approach, however, was to show that it is important to consider how one policy can have both positive and negative impacts on different stakeholders.

▸ When presented with any policy it is important to think carefully about these issues but also to consider how the policy as a whole fits with other policies and services.

▸ It is only through careful analysis that those to whom the policy applies will be able to take a more central role in the shaping of future policy as well as the implementation of current policy.

Further reading

To understand the impact of policy on practitioners, children and parents it is helpful to read documents and reports that may be aimed at each of these groups. A number of government publications, particularly from the Sure Start Unit, are relevant and their websites are listed at the end of the book. In addition, the following publications and website may be of interest:

HM Treasury/Department for Education and Skills/Department for Work and Pensions/Department of Trade and Industry (2004) *Choice for Parents, the Best Start for Children: A Ten-year Strategy for Childcare*, London: HMSO.

Provides a comprehensive overview of the intended direction of future policy in early years care and education and will be useful to readers.

Department of Health/DfES (Department for Education and Skills) (2004) *National Service Framework for Children, Young People and Maternity Services: Executive Summary*, London: Department of Health/DfES. Similarly lays out plans for health.

It is important, though, for readers to be aware that these are government intentions and they do not engage in a critical debate of the issues covered.

Children's Workforce Development Council, www.cwdcouncil.org.uk. The site contains details of development across the children's workforce sector.

Siraj-Blatchford, I., Taggart, B., Sylva, K., Sammons, P. and Melhuish, E. (2008) 'Towards the transformation of practice in early childhood education: the effective provision of preschool education (EPPE) project', *Cambridge Journal of Education*, 38(1): 23–36. The EPPE project has been a significant piece of research since 1997 and is likely to continue to be as it follows a large cohort of children through their primary education years. There are a number of publications from this project that will be useful to readers, but particularly the findings from the first phase, which tracked children through to the end of Key Stage 1. This paper outlines how EPPE investigated practice and identified how improvements can be achieved. It includes an in-depth discussion of the qualitative findings from settings identified as providing high standards of practice.

Analysing the Impact of Policy

Chapter 7

This chapter explains :

▶ a number of approaches that can be taken to analyse policy, and includes examples drawn from current policies to set this in a practice context and to promote an understanding of how drawing on research evidence and comparison with other countries can assist this analysis

▶ although some specific policy examples are used, the varied approaches to assist analysis and many of the questions posed would apply equally to the range of policies in early years services.

When analysing the potential impact of any policy it is important to look broadly. It can help to think about this in terms of completing a jigsaw puzzle. At the start you connect the edges. This gives an outline shape and some information about what the finished puzzle will look like, but it does not provide the whole picture. Over time you try different pieces together, move them around and gradually the whole picture starts to fall into place. By the time the puzzle is complete it is likely that you will have handled each of the pieces several times and will have thought carefully about how they fit together, and referred frequently to the box to compare the emerging puzzle and complete picture. Analysis is very similar to this. The pieces of the puzzle can be seen as representing policies. To gain a more in-depth understanding of different policies is difficult, but there are a number of approaches that you can take to help achieve this. Analysing policies is about looking at how they fit with current policies and practice, looking at how different parts of the policy impact on different stakeholders and how all this fits together in providing appropriate and responsive services for children, families and the wider community.

To analyse policy you can contrast current approaches with historical evidence, consider how policy impacts on varied stakeholders, consider themes running through different policies or contrast the approach in the countries of the UK with other countries. By drawing on one or more of these methods it is likely that you will be able to identify benefits and areas for development within policies and begin to gain a more analytical view of the impact of policy on the lives of children, parents and practitioners.

Why analyse policies?

Policy formation and implementation is a complex process that can take a considerable amount of time. A challenge for all policies is reconciling different priorities between those whom the policy will affect, such as practitioners, parents and children (National Audit Office, 2001). A number of different elements also need to be considered, including the implementation costs, the ability of services and service providers to deliver the policy aims, potential benefits, impact on different stakeholders and sustainability. Many policies aimed at children and families can cover a broad remit. For example, Children's Centres (many of which were former Sure Start local projects) bring together health, social services, education and voluntary services to respond to the requirements of individual families or sections of the community. It is also likely that the broader a policy, i.e. one which covers many policies in the area of children and family services, the more likely it is to impact not only on other people but also on other policies. A potential risk with this broad approach is that the policy may not benefit all those whom it is intended to benefit. Sanderson (2003) contrasts the approach of evidence-based practice and the belief in government departments that 'what counts is what works'. At a simple level this does not seem problematic. In the context of complex policies, though, it is likely that an approach to analysing policy that simply aims to say whether a policy is working or not working will not capture the true impact of the policy, which is likely to include positive and negative elements. Sanderson (2003) highlights other problems with this approach. What is meant by the term 'what works'? Just because a policy is working for a parent does not mean it works for a child, or a policy that works in one area will work in another. There is also a heavy government focus on measuring outcomes, usually through targets, but not everything is easily measurable or attributable to one specific policy. Since the change of prime minister, there have been signals that a broader approach to measuring policy/service outcomes, rather than service outcomes alone, will be implemented. However, this remains to be implemented across service providers. To overcome this, it is important to take a systematic and detailed approach to analysing the impact of policies that may provide the means to:

- ▶ decide if the information is accurate and how it will impact on practice
- ▶ argue why some aspects of policy are preferable to others
- ▶ identify aspects of good practice
- ▶ identify where there are shortcomings

- ▸ ensure high-quality services

- ▸ identify gaps in policy and service provision

- ▸ highlight how policy is meeting the requirements of different stakeholders

- ▸ offer a critical appraisal of a new approach to service delivery

- ▸ offer a critical appraisal of a local, regional, national or international policy.

Since 1997 a number of policies have been introduced into children and family services. The National Childcare Strategy set out the government's intention to increase provision across the maintained, voluntary and private sectors through a number of initiatives. Children's Trusts, which were implemented in most areas by 2006, aim to integrate locally based education, social services and some health services for children and young people (DfES/Department of Health, 2004). The Children's National Service Framework, set out long-term plans for sustained improvement in health from birth through to adulthood (Department of Health/DfES, 2004). More recently the Children's Plan (DCSF, 2007a) set out intentions to enhance the role of Children's Trusts, place schools at the centre of the community and integrate service provision; all with the aim of improving outcomes for children and families. These policies may be more accurately seen as a package of several programmes (NAO, 2001), which aim to provide equal opportunities and enhance the outcomes for each child and family. Consequently when analysing the impact of these policies it will be necessary to explore which objectives have been met, which have not and if all those intended to benefit from the policy have done or are likely to do so.

Levels of policy

Policies can be designed and implemented at different levels. National polices, which set out detailed arrangements, are often formulated in response to legislation. For example, the Children's Plan 2007 will lead to policies being implemented that will impact on the organization of children's services, strategies to improve the well-being of all children, and support to address the diverse needs of looked-after children. In response to this, organizations, local authority service providers and early years care and education settings may amend existing policies or implement new policies to ensure that working practices take account of new expectations, and potentially new legislation. Analysis can be carried out on policy at each of these levels. This approach can provide valuable information to see how far a policy is meeting the stated aims and objectives, and if the statements and philosophies of the policies are evident in practice (Fitzgerald, 2004).

Approaches to analysing the impact of policy

As seen in earlier chapters, policies can impact on different aspects of service provision and take time to become embedded. Policies can also be analysed at different stages – from initial design, at implementation, through to ongoing maintenance of the policy (NAO, 2001). Glass (2001) argues that when analysing what works it is necessary to think broadly. For example, when looking at poverty, policies that link to housing, quality of public services and the urban environment can all contribute to reducing poverty. The creation of Sure Start Children's Centres, Health Action Zones and the New Deal are all examples of policies that can contribute to tackling the impact of poverty on children and families in communities with high levels of deprivation and social exclusion. A clear challenge for any analysis of policy is to consider not only the benefits of individual policies, but also if different policies complement each other and enhance well-being or potentially if the complexity leads to confusion and a lack of clarity about the overall aims and objectives.

Does policy represent the perspectives of all stakeholders?

Most policies will impact on a range of stakeholders, including children, parents, practitioners and, often, members of the wider community. Policy can also create differences between stakeholders within the same category. For example, when changes were introduced to childminding, the increased professionalism and impact of regulation caused some childminders to stop working, and led to a significant decline in numbers. This was seen as a problem by some and as an advantage by others. When analysing the impact of policy it is important to consider if policies have succeeded or failed in addressing the diverse issues of the different stakeholders who are affected by the policy. Over the past decade the UNCRC could be seen as one vehicle that has helped policy to move beyond a welfare perspective. For children this has potentially positive benefits: it sees them as having rights as well as being the recipients of adult protection and places expectations on governments to ensure the rights of children are respected, addressed in policy and the outcome evaluated. The impact of this is that the interests of children should now be paramount in policy design and implementation, they should be able to exercise rights and their views should be consulted and acted upon (Lansdown, 2001). Although this may not happen in all instances, it does provide a basis on which an analysis of policy in respecting and promoting the right of children to be consulted can be assessed.

Activity

Read the following scenario, which describes a typical daily scene for almost every young child in England, and think carefully about the policies that the education provision is based on and how well each of them takes account of the perspective of the child.

Sarah is six years old and is in Year 1 with 28 other children. She is with some of her friends from the reception class but her best friend from reception is in the other Year 1 class. She has had some difficulties with reading and has one-to-one support from a teaching assistant three times a week to help her with reading.

She enjoys being at school but misses being able to play with different toys and outside on the bikes and climbing frame. Her favourite lesson is art as she likes to paint the people she has heard about in stories. Sarah likes to write some words on her paintings about the characters in stories and her teacher helps her to do this.

Initially it may seem that there are very few explicit policies here but this may be because so many policies are taken for granted. Each of the following aspects of policy or practice could potentially impact on Sarah:

▶ school starting age

▶ the National Curriculum

▶ the Primary Framework for literacy and mathematics

▶ special educational needs policy

▶ legal expectations placed on registered providers against which they are judged by inspectorate bodies in the UK

▶ school results targets

▶ the Primary National Strategy

▶ governing body decisions.

From this list the only clear reference to the need to consult children is contained in the Special Educational Needs Code of Practice (DfES, 2001), which emphasizes, 'the importance of finding out the ascertainable wishes and feelings of children and involving them when decisions are made that affect them' (section 4: 3). This would only apply if Sarah had been identified as having a special educational need, which may not be the case. The important point from this, however, is that just because there is an expectation, through the UNCRC, that children will be consulted, it does not automatically mean they will be, and this needs to be highlighted in any analysis of policy. Although the National Curriculum and the National Primary Strategy and the Literacy and Mathematics Frameworks may have strengths, it could be argued that the approach they dictate to learning is not the most appropriate for young children and it is likely that if consulted, children in Key Stage 1 would choose an approach to learning that resembles more closely that of the Early Years Foundation Stage (DfES, 2007b).

Generally speaking one of the areas in the UK where the impact of various policies is felt most by children is education, but it is potentially the area where their views have the least impact or are not considered at all. Even where children are consulted, however, this may not equate with their views being respected and acted upon. Tisdall and Davis (2004) raise questions about the effectiveness and ethical considerations of some approaches to consultation based around school councils and whether they lead to democratic communities. This is not meant to suggest that all attempts to consult children are flawed, but it does highlight the need to look systematically at the strategies that are in place to allow organizations to claim that children are consulted. The following questions clearly show how careful analysis can help to appraise the approaches in place to listen to and act upon the views of children:

▶ Do all children have the right to participate, or is participation focused on more articulate or older children?

▶ Do the approaches provide the basis for children to take on decision-making positions?

▶ Is consultation acted on or is it simply tokenistic?

▶ Is feedback provided to the representatives to show what progress has been made?

The Scottish Executive has undertaken a number of consultations with children, in areas such as school food (Shoolbread, 2006) and special educational needs (SEN) policy. The SEN review aimed to involve children at different stages of the process. This was achieved by consulting an initial group of 39 children, further consultation with a group of 46 children and young people, and finally questionnaires completed by a group of over 100 children and young people. The strengths of this process were that it included children with disabilities and those with English as an additional language, and the views of the respondents were used to inform policy-makers at early stages of policy design. During the process feedback was offered to each group but no regular involvement of children or young people in the policy development group was put in place, although this was asked for. Overall, the involvement of the children and young people led to some changes but there were limitations on what was implemented, which shows that imbalance of power between children and adults still existed (Tisdall and Davis, 2004). Even though there were still limitations in this approach, it does show how children can be involved and provides a basis for analysing whether the perspective of children is in evidence at policy design, implementation and maintenance stages. For England the Children's Plan made a greater attempt to include the views of children through the 'Time to Talk' consultation, which is a welcome development given that they are at the heart of planned developments and it is an area where England has been poor in the past.

Another example of how a major policy can impact on children is the changing role of classroom assistants. Their numbers have increased by over 100 per cent in eight years and this rise looks set to continue (Eyres et al., 2004). Initially, policies which have led to this (such as the National Literacy Strategy, increased inclusion of children with additional needs or disabilities in mainstream education, and initiatives to cut teacher workload) would seem to be beneficial. But has this increase only brought benefits and, if so, has everybody benefited?

Activity

Think about the increase in the number of support staff in early years and Key Stage 1. List some of the potential benefits and disadvantages of this policy for support staff, teaching staff and children.

Your benefits and disadvantages may have included some of the following:

Potential benefits	*Potential disadvantages*
Children receive more individual support	Some children become labelled as needing additional support from a young age
Increased employment opportunities for support	Reducing the professional status of the staff teaching role
Increased career opportunities for support staff	Changes driven by need to cut teacher workload rather than to increase career opportunities for support staff
Support for teachers as tasks can be shared among a team (increased work–life balance)	Support staff taking on roles that were previously teaching roles and are not paid at an equivalent level
Often brings opportunities for helpers from the community to take on paid roles	Limited access to appropriate training and a career framework to ensure progression opportunities

The fact that there are potential benefits and disadvantages with increasing the number of support staff in education does not mean that the policies that have led to this are bad. It does illustrate, though, that analysis of these points is important as it can highlight the potential advantages and disadvantages from the perspective of the different stakeholders that are affected and help to identify where further developments are necessary. Eyres et al. (2004) support many of these points as their research found that even young children were aware of the many different adults in nurseries or classrooms and found this generally helpful as long as there was a level of stability in staffing. In terms of how children saw these different people, they generally did not perceive significant differences in adults' roles within the classroom. It is difficult to speculate why, but this does raise issues around different pay scales, access to training and career opportunities. If the split between the role of the teacher and support staff is becoming harder to identify, there may be implications for workforce remodelling and the opportunities and challenges this brings in terms of pay and career structure. A response to many of these potential disadvantages could be addressed by the introduction of Higher Level Teaching Assistant (HLTA) or Early Years Professional Status, which, to be achieved, requires trainees to follow a recognized course of training. It is still far from clear what the policies that have led to these increases will mean in terms of progression and pay for those who have achieved the necessary standards to receive the award of HLTA (Teacher Training Agency, 2004). For the Early Years Professional role, which was introduced as part of the government commitment to have a graduate in every daycare setting by 2015, this issue is even more stark given that the status is seen as having equivalency to Qualified Teacher Status (QTS) standards (CWDC, 2007). Undoubtedly these roles, which encourage practitioners to enhance their skills, offer potential benefits, but to achieve the best from these policies careful evaluation will be needed to see how they benefit children, those pursuing the training and other practitioners who work in early years and school settings (Fitzgerald and Kay, 2008).

Parents have a pivotal role both within the family and when working in partnership with early years care and education settings. In addition they are stakeholders in many policies impacting on early years education and care. When parents and practitioners work together there can be significant benefits for them in terms of self-esteem and for children as they see a unified approach between the home and setting. This can also help practitioners to have a greater understanding and respect for each family (Fitzgerald, 2004). The approach of the government to families is about providing opportunities for them to lift themselves out of poverty and break down barriers that lead to social exclusion. To achieve these aims, policies have been implemented to increase childcare provision, offer financial support and ensure a minimum wage level (Roberts, 2001). It is also important to analyse whether there are implicit assumptions within policies, based on idealized images or assumptions of the family. In the past the government has championed marriage as the most stable environment for children to be raised in (Home Office, 1998), but many children flourish in non-traditional families (Patterson, 2006). Family relationships, the quality of parenting and levels of support are examples of important variables and show the potential negative impact of conveying certain types of family as second best (Roberts, 2001). Analysing the likelihood of policies to enhance these variables, rather than focusing on promoting one type of family structure above another, is clearly important.

Using past reports and service developments to appraise policy

Activity

Read through the overview of the Children's Plan and consider the following questions before reading this section:

▶ What are the potential positive impacts of the Children's Plan for children, parents and service providers?

▶ What are the potential negative impacts of the Children's Plan for children, parents and service providers?

▶ What evidence can be used to assess whether the targets set out in the Children's Plan have been achieved?

▶ What barriers may exist to achieving the targets set out in the Children's Plan and how could these be overcome?

▶ Are there any difficulties in accessing the overall impact of this national policy?

Children's Plan: Building brighter futures

The Plan, published at the end of 2007, outlines the government's strategy to further improve the lives of children and young people for the next 10 years. The Plan was developed through the national consultation.

Key points:

The Plan will be implemented between now and 2011 and proposes to:

▶ strengthen support for all families during the early years of their children's lives

▶ achieve 'world-class' schools and an excellent education for every child

▶ involve parents and carers fully in their children's learning

▶ provide more places for children to play safely.

This will be achieved through each of the outcomes of ECM by:

continued

Be healthy

- Review of CAMHS by the DCSF and NHS.
- Publication of a child health strategy.
- An assessment of the impact of the commercial world on children's well-being.

Stay safe

- Local authorities will be encouraged to create more 20 m.p.h. speed limit zones (particularly around play areas).
- Additional investment in new home safety equipment targeted at the most vulnerable families.
- A Staying Safe Action Plan will be published.

Enjoy and achieve

- Raise the entitlement to free nursery care for all three- and four-year-olds from 12 to 15 hours per week from 2010.
- Additional funding to ensure nurseries in the most disadvantaged areas have at least two graduates by 2015.
- Provide support for continuing professional development for practitioners in educare settings.
- Free childcare for 12,000 two-year-olds from disadvantaged families.
- A review of the primary national curriculum with changes implemented from September 2011.
- Additional resources to support the development of early writing, reading and counting.
- Implement 'stage not age' testing if the Making Good Progress trials evaluate successfully.
- Move towards a Master's-level teaching workforce and support for developing leadership skills.
- Provide up-to-date information to parents about their child's progress, attendance and behaviour.
- Additional investment to improve initial teacher training about special educational needs.
- A review into special education needs provision in 2009 following the review of language and communication that is taking place (Bercow Review).
- New guidance for building to ensure that schools are central to their communities through the collocation of child health services, social care, advice, welfare services and police.

continued

continued

▸ Build or upgrade more than 3,500 playgrounds (an average of 23 per local authority) and set-up 30 supervised play areas for children over eight.

▸ A new national play strategy.

Make a positive contribution

▸ Allocated funding over the three years to fund two new expert parenting advisers in every local authority.

▸ An expansion of family learning.

▸ Support young carers and deliver new support for families with disabled children.

Achieve economic well-being

▸ An action plan to tackle housing overcrowding and prioritize children's needs in housing decisions.

The principles of the Children's Plan and the emphasis it places on high-quality health, education and social experiences are vitally important for families and have the potential to have a significant positive impact on children's development (DCSF, 2007a). Evidence to support this analysis can be drawn from research and evaluations of service provision. For example, findings from the EPPE project support the aims of the Children's Plan in terms of providing early years care and education for children and emphasize the need to ensure it is of high quality through the provision of a highly skilled workforce (Sylva et al., 2004). The *Early Years Foundation Stage* (DfES, 2007a) and the *Key Elements of Effective Practice* (DfES/Sure Start, 2005) support many of the principles by emphasizing the need for equal and inclusive access for all children, the need to provide well-structured and appropriate play-based experiences, and the importance of working in partnership with parents. For families, particularly where there is only one adult in the household, strategies to make childcare more adaptable and affordable are likely to be beneficial. There are also wider implications for communities in terms of increased employment opportunities within the childcare workforce. A commitment to ensure there is appropriate training and ongoing support to ensure well-qualified and motivated staff is seemingly given. All in all the policy sets out a number of ambitious plans that would seem to be welcome to all families with children.

However, the National Childcare Strategy (1998), which can be seen as the preceding overall approach to education and care, set out to improve the number of childcare places and accessibility but this did not result in a similar level of provision in all parts of the UK. The targeted approach of providing additional resources for deprived areas has two significant flaws: it adds to the already fragmented and confusing array of provision within early years and it wrongly assumes that the 20–30 per cent of most deprived families live in the corresponding 20–30 per cent most deprived areas. Some areas have a number of maintained settings, which often include trained teachers who can have a positive impact on overall levels of quality (Sylva et al., 2004). Other areas have a number of integrated Children's Centres, where parents are able to access a range of support services for members of the family. The government has recognized the importance of providing joined-up services with the announcement of the expansion of Children's Centres to one in every community by 2010 (HM Treasury et al., 2004), but even with this, the majority of children will not receive early years care and education in this type of integrated provision (DCSF, 2008). A potential difficulty with any national policy, however, is that it may propose similar responses for all families. But children and families are not a homogenous group and policies need to be able to take account of this. Ongoing funds also need to be available to deliver the service and to carry out a systematic evaluation of the benefits it brings (Ghate, 2001). The emphasis on children and families has certainly risen on the political agenda since 1997 and is likely to remain high, whichever party forms the government, but *more* provision does not necessarily equate to *better* provision. To be clear, if there are benefits to increased provision, Ghate (2001) argues the importance of systematic evaluation that includes the views of service users and providers. In addition, as the number of Children's Centres grows they are likely to develop in different ways and a policy concentrating on increased provision does not automatically equate with increased quality.

Perhaps the most fundamental question that policies need to address is 'What works for children?' The Treasury response to this has been to impose a number of public service agreements on departments to ensure there are clear accountability measures in place. For example, Sure Start, which has the aim of improving health and well-being and lifting families out of poverty, has attracted large amounts of funding to help meet the targets set out in the National Childcare Strategy, many of which are reiterated in the Children's Plan. The Plan also assumes that all families will prefer to access early years care and education rather than care for their child at home. Some families may decide that caring for their child at home is their preferred option but there is far less support available for this choice. This may result in some families, perhaps because of lower income levels, feeling they have no choice but to return to work, as they are not able to manage financially.

To assess whether the targets set out in the Children's Plan will be achieved a range of evidence could be used. Government statistics about the number of early years care and education places, levels of poverty and the average cost of childcare could help to make an assessment. Reports from the Early Years Directorate of Ofsted can look at quality in specific settings and more generally across the sector. Information from evaluations and early years organizations could also be useful. For example, the Joseph Rowntree Foundation highlighted how early years care and education provision has improved but families still face a range of logistical difficulties in accessing provision because it is often provided in different locations and at times that do not fit easily with work patterns or the needs of different children (Joseph Rowntree Foundation, 2003). Although this relates to past provision, older evidence can be useful as, when contrasted with more recent evidence, it helps to evaluate the success of a policy over time rather than making a simple judgement that there has been either a complete success or complete failure. The content of provision can also be assessed for quality. It could be argued that a positive development for the early years care and education sector was the introduction of *Birth to Three Matters* (for children from birth to three) (Sure Start Unit, 2002) and the *Curriculum Guidance for the Foundation Stage* (for children from three to six) (QCA/DfEE, 2000) as they take account of the developmental needs of young children and promote an appropriate curriculum. In contrast, the introduction of these two separate curriculum documents and the formal approach of the Key Stage 1 curriculum could be seen as adding to, rather than reducing, the fragmentation of the sector. An alternative response to this could have been to introduce one curriculum that addressed the developmental needs and well-being of children in the early years, similar to the approach being developed in Wales. This also offers a potential comparison with which to analyse the English system (Welsh Assembly, 2004). Although there is still a divide between the early years curriculum and Key Stage 1 in England, contrasting past developments with the recent introduction of a combined early years curriculum (Early Years Foundation Stage) demonstrates how evidence over a period of time can help to make a detailed analysis of progress to date and identify, with the support of evidence, where further development could be beneficial.

Overall there are likely to be benefits that are the direct result of the Children's Plan although it can be difficult to accurately assess these. For example, since 2000 there has been a reduction in child poverty, fewer deaths of children due to injury, lower levels of infant and child mortality and an increase in the number of infants being breast fed. Alongside this there has been a rise in childhood obesity, increased levels of asthma and diabetes and a reduction in the number of children being immunized against measles (Bradshaw, 2002). Within different communities there may have been a number of policies operating, such as Sure Start, neighbourhood renewal initiatives, educational projects, New Deal, Health Action Zones, Primary National Strategy and the Healthy Schools Initiative, which can make it difficult to attribute change to one specific policy. This is discussed by Kurtz in relation to conflicting evidence between policies that aim to reduce social exclusion and the different explanations that can be linked to rises in specific disorders, which 'indicates the complexities in interpreting the relationship between overall national trends in health indicators and policy initiatives'

(2003: 176). Although health measures do not relate directly to the Children's Plan, it does clearly highlight the need for caution in attributing specific change to one national policy without the evidence to link outcomes with implementation initiatives. Based on this it could also be argued that an analysis of any national policy, especially in terms of assessing whether targets have been achieved, is best undertaken through local evaluations that are more able to identify specific benefits and disadvantages in the context of the range of policy initiatives that are likely to be in place.

Approaches to analyse policy: evaluative themes

A range of questions can be asked to promote the analysis of policy. Dowling (1999) suggests that commitment to early years care and education can be seen in terms of four broad themes: insufficiency, diversity, lack of resources and commitment. To analyse the impact of policy, questions can be asked that relate to the level of commitment in terms of provision and resources to implement policy plans at a regional and local level. They can relate to how likely policies are to lead to integrated, high-quality provision for each child and family. This approach to analysing policy can be applied at different levels, for example to evaluate a broad government policy (for example, the Children's Plan) or the implementation of policy within a setting (for example, implementing the Special Educational Needs Code of Practice in a nursery setting).

The framework suggests a number of questions in different areas that could be applied to evaluate policy. It is unlikely, and perhaps unnecessary, that all of the questions would be applied to one policy. Decisions will need to be made about what is being evaluated and the purpose of the analysis. If it is for an essay, which is aiming to contrast the approach of central governments pre- and post-1997 to early years care and education, it is likely that a number of commitment and resource questions will be raised. If the aim is to evaluate the level of participation of families and children in issues that affect them in their nursery, the focus may be on questions drawn from the diversity section.

The following questions are not meant to be seen as a definitive response to achieving a comprehensive analysis of policy. They could be seen as offering a starting point to promote in-depth analysis, a stimulus to add a critical dimension to analysing policies, or as a vehicle to promote critical discussion of specific issues. If the aim is to offer a broad overview, it may be useful to include discussion of questions from each section. For a more in-depth analysis of an aspect of policy, questions may be drawn mainly from one area. It is also likely that the initial questions asked would do two things: provide answers and raise more questions.

Commitment

▸ Is there clear leadership at national, regional and local levels?

▸ Is there a commitment to integrated services and strategies in place to achieve this?

▸ Is there evidence of commitment across central departments and professions to developing integrated services for children and families?

▸ Are messages from research being integrated into policy and practice to raise the quality of early years care and education services?

▸ Is there a commitment to increase the level and quality of early years care and education services?

▸ Is there commitment to promoting the involvement of children and families in service planning and evaluation?

Insufficiency

▸ Does the level of provision match demand in all areas of the UK?

▸ Are there sufficient early years care and education places for all children who require them?

▸ Are there differences between urban and rural locations?

▸ Does the timing of provision match the needs of children and families?

▸ Are there an adequate number of practitioners with appropriate qualifications?

▸ Are there policies/plans in place to overcome any gaps in insufficiency?

Resources

▸ Does the level of resources from central government recognize and allow the development of the early years care and education sector?

▸ How are resources being allocated and shared at a local level?

▸ Are resources being increased over time to allow the development of early years care and education provision?

▸ Are resources sustainable in the long term, particularly outside the maintained sector?

▸ Are resources appropriate to the requirements of service users?

Diversity

▸ Does the range of provision meet the diverse requirements of children and families?

▸ Do all children and families have equal access to provision?

▸ What support and training are available to practitioners to ensure they have the skills to respond to all children and families?

▸ Do policies value and promote the integration of each child and family?

▸ Are providers aware of the diversity of family structures and do they respond to this appropriately?

▸ Are the voices of each child and family heard equally?

International evidence

Several countries now have policy initiatives similar to those of the UK, which are aimed at providing services that respond to the requirements of children and families, particularly those with lower income levels. Another similarity of many of these countries with the UK is the emphasis on preventative responses which address all aspects of support that families may need through the provision of joined-up services (Vimpani, 2002). This evidence can provide another approach to analysing the likely impact of UK policy and providing a forum to debate the potential impacts of approaches that are similar to those in other countries.

In the USA there has been an increase in both the number of children using day-care facilities and the duration of time they spend there. In response to this the issue of quality has arisen, but in the absence of a national plan, such as the Children's Plan, individual states have responded in different ways. But evidence of the importance of high-quality environments from the USA is very similar to the UK: the higher the quality of the setting the better the cognitive, linguistic and social outcomes for children. High-quality indicators include high child/staff ratios, higher levels of qualified staff, knowledge of child development and positive interactions between staff and children. In contrast, research shows that most aspects of provision were of medium to poor quality (Grisham Brown and Hallam, 2004). An important message from this is that just because it is known what contributes to good quality, it cannot be assumed that this will be evident in day-to-day practice. The direction can be set out in policy documents but this will then require substantial effort to embed the principles of the policy into practice. Another important message to come out of the evaluation was the importance of consulting day-care providers to get an accurate reflection of early care and education initiatives (Grisham Brown and Hallam, 2004). Questions can be asked about how this compares with the UK and may suggest that revisions to quality assurance processes and evaluations are needed to take more account of the views of practitioners. Another contributing factor to quality, possibly the most significant, is the skills, knowledge and experience of the workforce. This is clearly recognized by the government as the Children's Plan contains a number of initiatives aimed at raising the skill base and career development opportunities of the workforce. In a number of countries, particularly across Europe, there are a significant number of pedagogues who are generally trained to graduate level, have both rhetorical and practical training combined, and work throughout a range of child and family services (OECD, 2006). Initially it may seem that this evidence could not be useful to help evaluate planned workforce developments in parts of the UK. However, it can offer a platform to compare the similarities and differences that this may have with similar roles in the UK (such as Early Years Professionals or Children's Centre Leaders), which could provide evidence to form a position on how successful ongoing or planned policy developments will prove.

In Australia the development of early childhood services has followed a similar path to that of the UK. There has been a heavy educational focus on policy and varied initiatives have caused an arbitrary division between caring and teaching. This has led to differences in levels of training, qualifications and philosophies underpinning service provision, which in many respects remain evident. Kindergarten provision, which children usually access the year before school, is seen to be good and has an educational focus. In contrast, childcare and day care is seen to be aimed at the socially disadvantaged and about meeting health and safety needs of children (Jillian, 1996). Evidence of this arbitrary division and the unsystematic development of early years services mirrors the historical development of UK services and provides comparisons to analyse the potential impact for current policies to move to less fragmented and more integrated early years services. The levels of early years care and education offered in Australia also have some similarities with the targeted approach of providing Sure Start local projects in England, which may result in less advantaged communities feeling stigmatized and raises questions about the need for a national childcare policy that leads to national levels of provision. What is clear, though, from international evidence is that a long-term policy commitment, backed by appropriate funding, will be necessary to bring about sustainable improvements in early years care and education in the UK, and this may not always sit easily alongside the quick-fix approach to societal issues (Vimpani, 2002).

International evidence can be useful for analysing approaches to child and family policy in the UK. Glass (2001) argues that caution needs to be applied if there is an unquestioned assumption that what works in other countries can be directly applied in UK contexts. In addition, there are differences within many aspects of policy between the countries of the UK and this was discussed in Chapter 6. There are likely to be aspects of policy, such as service design and raising the quality of early years care and education provision, that will work, but others may not. Any analysis of policy should consider this and ask what aspects of policy are transferable and what may be culture dependent. For example, the approach to funding in the USA is very different to the UK and introducing a policy that works well there may not achieve the same outcomes here. When using international evidence to appraise UK policy, as well as asking 'what works?', Glass (2001) suggests there is another fundamental question that needs to be considered: what is worth doing for children?

Summary ▢

▸ Analysing policy is a complex process, particularly in the area of early years as policies have become increasingly complex.

▸ Nonetheless, it is important to be able to make an appraisal of the broad issues and how they are likely to impact on the various stakeholders (including those whom polices are intended to have an impact on and those who may be affected indirectly).

▸ To assist readers with this process the chapter has suggested a number of approaches that can be helpful. It is by no means the only way to undertake analysis of policies but it is hoped that it provides a starting point and may generate other ideas. The approaches outlined included:

– measuring the effectiveness of polices according to outcomes (for example, how many additional childcare places have been created and how long these have been sustained for)

– assessing the ability of a policy to represent the perspective of different stakeholders, particularly children who may not be empowered through policy

– a comparison with past developments and evaluation reports

– assessing the approach of policy against research evidence (for example, examining whether the pedagogical approach of early years curricula is developmentally appropriate for young children)

– evaluating policy against a range of themes, including the level of commitment from government and policy-makers, the level of resources allocated to implementation and sustainability and the ability of the policy to respond to the diversity of stakeholders

– comparison with international approaches and evidence, but with attention to the level of transferability within the context of the UK and the policy approach in operation.

Further reading

One of the best ways to feel more confident with evaluating policy is to read widely to gain an understanding of how authors have approached the evaluation of policy. An approach to evaluating early years policy can be informed by reading magazines such as *Community Care* and newspapers such as the *Guardian* and the *Independent*, all of which can also be found online.

Roberts, M. (2001) 'Childcare policy', in P. Foley, J. Roche and S. Tucker (eds), *Children in Society: Contemporary Theory, Policy and Practice*, Basingstoke: Palgrave. Provides a useful overview of how the international context, through the UNCRC, has had an increasingly significant impact on policy design and implementation in the UK. Any evaluation of UK policy will need to take account of this.

Another important consideration is how well the views of children are taken account of in policy design and implementation. There is a general consensus that children are now more involved but this may not always be the case.

Tisdall, E.K.M. and Davis, J. (2004) 'Making a difference? Bringing children's and young people's views into policy making', *Children and Society*, 18(2): 131–42. Discusses a range of issues around the involvement of children and considers at what stages their views are taken account of and most importantly the impact that this involvement has.

Finally the most significant challenge for any policy is translating into practice the aspirations it outlines. This is relevant to the majority of policies within child and family services, particularly in the way services are organized and the implications this has for practitioners. In response to this, the following text discusses the impact of a range of early years policies on the workforce and the challenges this poses for service organization, training and development and working practices.

Fitzgerald, D. and Kay, J. (2008) *Working Together in Children's Services*, Oxford: Routledge.

Concluding Comments

In this second edition we discussed what early years policy is, how it has developed over time, what influences the development of policy and how it is implemented, evaluated and analysed. The development of early years policy has been particularly prolific since 1997 when early years issues became central to the government agenda. This has posed challenges in the study of early years in terms of understanding the range and complexity of policies affecting young children and their families. This emphasis on early years policy seems likely to continue into the future as the main political parties have all placed children and families firmly at the heart of their agendas. Recent developments in policy affecting young children are the most radical for over 30 years, involving wide-ranging changes to structures and practices in children's services. The impact of these developments on service provision is likely to be significant for years to come.

A complex range of factors, which combine to create change, influences policy development. These include historical influences, the perceived effectiveness of existing policy and the impact of lobbying by statutory and voluntary sector children's organizations. However, the key factor is the perceived importance of early years issues for the government of the day. This in turn is influenced by many interrelated factors, including meeting wider policy commitments, the role of individual ministers and senior civil servants, and the relationship between key figures in government and the early years sector.

Implementing policy at national and local government levels involves legislating for some areas of policy, disseminating information and guidance, and a comprehensive debate about how policy will work at ground level. The shape of policy is confirmed through these processes and the extent to which there is agreement between policy-makers and those delivering policy at service level. Modern policy-making is based on principles that should produce robust, effective developments that are informed by research evidence and lessons from the past. However, recent policies influencing early years have been large and complex and what exactly the eventual outcomes for children, families and practitioners will be remains unclear.

As the complexity of policy has increased it has become important when evaluating policy to consider the impact it has on the various stakeholders. For example, policies may have differing impacts on parents and children. A policy to support parents returning to work may improve their employability and income but result in children spending longer in day care. Similarly, policies that have led to significant expansion in the provision of early years services have not, so far, led to increased access to training for all practitioners, recognition of their skills and experience and the implementation of a systematic career framework to promote progression. Nonetheless, as highlighted, there are potentially plans in place to address some of these issues, which emphasize the need for ongoing evaluation.

The remit of this second edition is to help readers understand their own role in policy development as practitioners, employees and members of children's organizations. Policy is the product of human activity and as such can be influenced by those involved. As stated in Chapter 1, practitioners need to understand policy in terms of how it determines their roles and responsibilities, the structures and policies of their workplaces, and the quality of service provision to children and families. Throughout the book the content and activities have provided a basis to help the reader engage with the complexity of policy-making, implementation and evaluation across the UK. Chapter 5 deals with the current similarities and differences between policy in the UK countries. However, as policy develops continually, it is very important to develop strategies for keeping up to date with new initiatives. This second edition provides you with a range of tools to understand and evaluate policy, but keeping up to date is your responsibility.

Glossary

This glossary contains explanations of terms that may not be familiar to the reader. Terms which are used in the text but fully explained or discussed so their meaning is clear are not included.

Area Child Protection Committee (ACPC): multi-agency committees established in every local authority to determine local policy and oversee child protection processes. ACPCs have been replaced by **Local Safeguarding Children Boards**, which are statutory bodies introduced by the Children Act 2004.

Birth to Three Matters: a framework of effective practice for those working with children aged birth to three issued by the Department for Education and Skills (DfES). This was replaced by the **Early Years Foundation Stage** (birth to six years) in 2008.

Children's Centres: currently based in the 20 per cent most disadvantaged wards in England, although the plan is to expand to over 3,500 centres by 2010. Children's Centres provide early education integrated with full day care, identification of and provision for children with special educational needs and disabilities, parental outreach, family support, and health services, among others.

Children's Trusts: multi-agency bodies established to ensure that joint planning and implementation of plans for children and young people within local authorities are effective. The philosophy of Children's Trusts is underpinned by the Children Act 2004 duty to cooperate and to focus on improving outcomes for all children and young people.

Civil Service: in Great Britain the Civil Service helps the government of the UK, the Scottish Executive and the National Assembly for Wales formulate their policies, carry out decisions and administer public services for which they are responsible. Civil servants are servants of the Crown, meaning the government of the UK, the Scottish Executive and the National Assembly for Wales.

Curriculum Guidance for the Foundation Stage: statutory guidance for early years practitioners in the Foundation Stage (three to five years) on developing a curriculum to support teaching and learning towards the Early Learning Goals. This was replaced by the **Early Years Foundation Stage** (birth to six years) in 2008.

Daycare Trust: a national childcare charity established in 1980, campaigning for high-quality affordable childcare for all.

Desirable Learning Outcomes: learning goals that set out what children should have achieved by the time they entered compulsory education. These were replaced by the **Early Learning Goals**.

Early Excellence Centres: early years settings that have been highlighted as offering a level of excellence. These became rebranded as Children's Centres.

Early Learning Goals: the basis of the Foundation Stage curriculum in any early years setting in England.

Early Years Foundation Stage: the statutory curriculum for children aged from birth to six.

Early Years Professional Status (EYPS): is a graduate status that can be achieved by following one of the recognized training or validation pathways to demonstrate a range of skills and attributes. EYPS is seen as having equivalence with Qualified Teacher Status.

Early Years Professionals (EYPs): the aim of Early Years Professionals is to lead effective high-quality practice in the early years sector. The government's aim is to have at least one EYP in every early years setting by 2015.

Foundation Stage: the curriculum in England, for children aged from birth to six years (see **Early Years Foundation Stage**).

Local Government Association (LGA): formed in 1997 to represent the 500 local authorities of England and Wales and to promote better local government.

Local Safeguarding Children Boards: multi-disciplinary statutory bodies responsible for child protection issues in each local authority (see **Area Child Protection Committees**).

National Childminding Association (NCMA): promotes and supports quality childminding expertise, provides information for parents looking for childminders, and provides information and news updates for childminders.

Office for Standards in Education (Ofsted): a non-ministerial government department established under the Education (Schools) Act 1992, Ofsted has expanded over time and now takes responsibility for the inspection of all schools, LEAs, teacher training institutions, youth work, colleges, and early years childcare and education provision in England.

Pre-school Learning Alliance (PLA): an educational charity that represents and supports 15,000 community pre-schools in England.

Primary care trusts: 302 free-standing statutory bodies that control local health care and receive their budgets directly from the Department of Health.

Private sector: refers to the business or profit-making sector providing services in the early years, for example, private day nurseries and childminders.

Public sector: refers to the local or central government sector providing services in the early years, for example, schools.

standard assessment tests (SATS): are completed at the end of Key Stage 1, 2 and 3 to assess progress in the core subjects of the National Curriculum. At Key Stage 1, they now take a less formal style, with schools having a choice of when pupils complete the assessment tasks. They are also referred to as National Curriculum tests.

Sure Start local programmes: an area-based initiative with the aim of improving the health and well-being of families and children from before birth to four. There were 524 programmes in neighbourhoods where a high proportion of children lived in poverty. The majority have now been transformed into **Children's Centres**.

Sure Start Unit: part of the Children, Young People and Families Directorate in the Department for Children, Schools and Families (DCFS), working with a wide range of other agencies to develop services for children and families in line with government policy, including services to socially excluded children and families.

Universal services: available to all in a stated category (not means-tested), for example, child benefit is available to all families with children.

Voluntary sector: non-government or profit-making charitable or voluntary organizations such as the NSPCC and Barnardo's.

Useful Websites

As explained throughout the book, policy is constantly developing and new initiatives being trialled or implemented. One way to keep up to date with policy developments is to consult websites from government departments, professional organizations and other relevant bodies. In addition to the websites mentioned in the text, the following websites are likely to be helpful in this task:

4 Nations Child Policy Network: www.childpolicy.org.uk/enghome/index.cfm
Contains information about recent policy developments in the four nations of the UK.

Children's services in the Department of Health: www.dh.gov.uk/PolicyAndGuidance/HealthAndSocialCareTopics/ChildrenServices/fs/en
Details current government policy and initiatives in health and related services.

Daycare Trust: www.daycaretrust.org.uk/
National childcare charity with information and responses to policy developments in childcare.

Department for Children, Schools and Families: www.dcsf.gov.uk/
Details current government policy and initiatives in education and employment.

Department of Trade and Industry: www.dti.gov.uk/
Contains information on work–life balance, parental leave and issues relevant to working parents.

Every Child Matters: www.everychildmatters.gov.uk
Provides information about policy developments and new initiatives.

Joseph Rowntree Foundation: www.jrf.org.uk/
Social policy research charity that produces reports on a range of social policy issues, including issues relevant to children and families.

National Children's Bureau: www.ncb.org.uk/
Provides comment, analysis and overview of issues relevant to children.

National Family and Parenting Institute: www.nfpi.org.uk/
A charity offering comment and advice to support parents bringing up their children.

Ofsted Childcare and Early Education: www.ofsted.gov.uk/portal/site/Internet/
menuitem.f08cb1ee80767b23b218d71008c08a0c/?vgnextoid=0da88487a73dc
010VgnVCM1000003507640aRCRD
Provides information about current issues for the registration, regulation and monitoring of early years provision.

Qualification and Curriculum Authority: www.qca.org.uk
Information about the Early Years Foundation Stage.

In addition, some of the websites above also offer the facility to receive regular email updates on new developments. This is an invaluable way of keeping abreast of ongoing policy developments.

References

Anning, A. (2004) 'The co-construction of an early childhood curriculum', in A. Anning, J. Cullen and M. Fleer (eds), *Early Childhood Education: Society and Culture*, London: Sage.

Ariès, P. (1960) *L'enfant et la vie familiale sous l'ancien régime*, Paris: Librairie Plon. Translated by R. Baldick (1962) as *Centuries of Childhood*, London: Jonathan Cape.

Arnold, R. (2005) *Early Years Childcare and Education – the Sure Start Agenda: the Beacon Council Scheme Round 5*, Windsor: NFER.

Artiles, A. and Dyson, A. (2005) 'Inclusive education in the globalisation age', in D. Mitchell (ed.), *Contextualising Inclusive Education – Evaluating Old and New International Perspectives*, London: Routledge.

Ashrof, H. (2005) 'The bigger picture on the Children Act, 2004', *Community Care*. Last accessed on 17 January 2008 at www.communitycare.co.uk/articles/article/asp?/liarticleid=47713&lisectionID=22&skeys="BiggerPicture"+Children+Act&liParentID=26

Association of Directors of Social Services (ADSS) (2005) *Consultation on Draft Statutory Guidance on the Role and Responsibilities of the Director of Children's Services and Lead Member for Children's Services*. Last accessed on 20 March 2005 at: www.adss.org.uk/publications/consresp/2005/children.shtml

Aubrey, C. (2004) 'Implementing the foundation stage in reception classrooms', *British Educational Research Journal*, 30(5): 633–56.

Audit Commission (2002) 'Statuatory Assessment and Statements of SEN: In Need of Review?' London: TSO.

Baldock, P. (2001) *Regulating Early Years Services*, London: David Fulton.

Barnardos (2003) *'Green Paper* "Every Child Matters"', 8 September. Last accessed on 1 March 2005 at: www.barnardos.org.uk/newsandevents/media/press/release.jsp?id=1153

BBC (2008a) *Child Protection Plans 'failing'*, BBC News channel, 22 January 2008. Last accessed on 30 July 2008 at: http://news.bbc.co.uk/1/hi/programmes/file_on_4/7200217.stm

References

BBC (2008b) *Call to Scrap Children's Database*, BBC News channel, 21 February 2008. Last accessed on 7 July 2008 at: http://news.bbc.co.uk/1/hi/uk_politics/7256972.stm

Bell, A. and La Valle, I. (2005) *Early Stages of the Neighbourhood Nurseries Initiative: Parents' Experiences*, London: DFES/Sure Start Unit.

Bilton, H. (1998) *Outdoor Play in the Early Years: Management and Innovation*, London: David Fulton.

Bradshaw, J. (ed.) (2002) *The Well-being of Children in the UK*, London: University of York and Save the Children.

Brandon, M., Howe, A., Dagley, V., Salter, C., Warren, C., Black, J. (2006) 'Evaluating the common assessment framework and lead professional guidance and implementation in 2005–6'. DfES Research Report RR740 University of East Anglia.

Brannen, J. and Moss, P. (eds) (2003) *Rethinking Children's Care*, Buckingham: Open University Press.

Bromley, C., Curtice, J., McCrone, D. and Park, A. (eds) (2006) *Has Devolution Delivered?* Edinburgh: Edinburgh University Press.

Brooks, G., Cook, M., Hadden, S., Hirst, K., Jones, S., Lever-Chain, J., Millman, L., Piech, B., Powell, S., Rees, F., Roberts, S. and Smith, D. (2004) *Early Promise: The University of Sheffield National Evaluation of Early Start for the Basic Skills Agency*, London: Basic Skills Agency.

Bruce, T. (2001) 'The north and south divided', *Nursery World*, 12 July: 34.

Children's Workforce Development Council (CWDC) (2007) *Prospectus: Early Years Professional Status*. Last accessed on 15 March 2008 at: www.cwdcouncil.org.uk/pdf/Early%20Years/EYP_Prospectus_0407.pdf

Children's Workforce Network (2008) *Integrated Qualifications Framework*, CWN. www.cwdcouncil.org.uk/iqf, accessed 7 October 2008.

Clark, M.M. and Waller, T. (eds) (2007) *Early Childhood Education & Care: Policy and Practice'*, London: Sage Publications.

Cleaver, H., Barnes, J., Bliss, D. and Cleaver, D. (2004) 'Developing Information Sharing and Assessment Systems'. Nottingham: DfES Publications.

Community Care (2004) 'Hearts and minds reluctantly follow as bill finally completes passage', 1549, 18 November: 18–19.

Community Care (2005) 'A clash of cultures?', 1660, 17 February: 4.

Croll, P. and Moses, D. (2000) *Special Needs in the Primary School: One in Five?* London: Continuum.

Crowe, B. (1973) *The Playgroup Movement*, London: George Allen and Unwin.

Cunningham, H. (2006) *The Invention of Childhood*, London: BBC Books.

Dahlberg, G., Moss, P. and Pence, A. (1999) *Beyond Quality in Early Childhood*

Education and Care: Postmodern Perspectives, London: Falmer Press.

David, T. (ed.) (1994) *Working Together for Young Children: Multi-professionalism in action*, London: Routledge.

Dawson, H. (2004) 'The Children Act obstacle course', *Community Care*, 1552, 9 December: 24.

Daycare Trust (2005) 'Childcare and early years services in 2004', paper 1 of *A New Era for Universal Childcare?* Last accessed on 15 March 2005 at: daycaretrust.org.uk

Deloitte and Touche (2008) *ContactPoint Data Security Review Executive Summary*, London: DCFS. Last accessed on 7 July at: www.parliament.uk/deposits/depositedpapers/2008/DEP2008–0502.pdf

Department for Children, Schools and Families (DCSF) (2007) *The Children's Plan: Building Brighter Futures*, Norwich: The Stationery Office.

Department for Children, Families and Schools (DCSF) (2008a) *Graduate Leader Fund: Further Information on Purpose and Implementation.* Last accessed on 2 July 2008 at: www.everychildmatters.gov.uk/earlyyearsworkforce/

Department for Children, Families and Schools (DCSF) (2008b) *Building Brighter Futures: Next Steps for the Children's Workforce.* DCSF: Nottingham.

Department for Education and Employment/School Curriculum and Assessment Authority (DfEE/SCAA) (1996) *Desirable Outcomes for Children's Learning on Entering Compulsory Education*, London: DFEE/SCAA.

DfEC (1993) The Special Educational Needs Codes of Practice. London: TSO.

Department for Education and Skills (DfES) (2001) *SEN Toolkit*, Nottinghamshire: DfES Publications.

Department for Education and Skills (DfES) (2001) *The Special Educational Needs Codes of Practice.* London: TSO

Department for Education and Skills (DfES) (2003) *Every Child Matters* (Green Paper), London: HMSO.

Department for Education and Skills (DfES) (2004a) *Every Child Matters: Next Steps*, London: DfES.

Department for Education and Skills (DfES) (2004b) *Every Child Matters: Change for Children*, London: HMSO.

Department for Education and Skills (DfES)/Department for Health (2004) *Children's Trusts.* Last accessed on 1 December 2004 at: www.dfes.gov.uk/childrenstrusts/

Department for Education and Skills (DfES) (2006) *Sure Start Children's Centres Planning and Performance Management Guidance.* Last accessed on 30 June 2008 at: http://publications.everychildmatters.gov.uk/eOrderingDownload/SSCC-PERFORM2006.pdf

Department for Education and Skills (DfES) (2007a) *Statutory Framework for*

References

the Early Years Foundation Stage, Nottingham: DfES.

Department for Education and Skills (DfES) (2007b) *Provision for Children Under Five Years of Age in England: January 2007.* Last accessed on 3 April 2008 at: www.dcsf.gov.uk/rsgateway/DB/SFR/s000729/SFR19–2007.pdf

Department for Education and Skills/Local Government Association (DfES/LGA) (2001) *Childcare and Early Education – Investing in All Our Futures,* London: DfES.

Department for Education Skills (DfES)/SureStart (2005) *Primary National Strategy: Key Elements of Effective Practice,* Norwich: HMSO.

Department of Education and Science (DES) (1967) *Children and Their Primary Schools* (Plowden Report), London: HMSO.

Department of Education and Science (DES) (1990) *Starting with Quality: Report of the Committee of Inquiry into the Educational Experiences Offered to Three and Four Year Olds* (Rumbold Report), London: HMSO.

Department of Health (1991) *The Children Act 1989: Guidance and Regulations.* Volume 2: *Family Support, Day Care and Educational Provision for Young Children,* London: HMSO.

Department of Health (1995) *Child Protection: Messages from Research,* London: HMSO.

Department of Health (1998) *Quality Protects: Framework for Action,* London: Department of Health.

Department of Health (1999) *Working Together to Safeguard Children,* London: HMSO.

Department of Health/Department for Education and Skills (DfES) (2004) *National Service Framework for Children, Young People and Maternity Services: Executive Summary,* London: Department of Health/DfES.

Department of Health/Welsh Office (1997) *People Like Us – the Report of the Review of Safeguards for Children Living Away from Home* (Utting Report), London: HMSO.

Department of Trade and Industry (DTI) (2004) *Work–Life Balance and Flexible Working – the Business Case.* Last accessed on 1 March 2005 at: www.dti.gov.uk/bestpractice/assets/wlb.pdf

Department of Trade and Industry (DTI) (2005) *Work and Families: Choice and Flexibility.* Last accessed on 1 March 2005 at: www.dti.gov.uk/er/workandfamilies.htm

Dowling, M. (1999) 'Early years: then, now and next', *Education 3–13,* 27(3): 5–10.

Dyson, A. (2005) 'Philosophy, politics and economics? The story of inclusive education in England', in D. Mitchell (ed.), *Contextualising Inclusive Education – Evaluating Old and New International Perspectives,* London: Routledge.

Elfer, P. (1997) *Attachment Theory and Day Care for Young Children*, Highlight series no.155, London: National Children's Bureau.

Elfer, P., Selleck, D. and Goldschmied, E. (2003) *Key Persons in the Nursery*, London: David Fulton.

Elliott, F. (2007) 'Safety fears over new register of all children', *The Times*, 27 August.

End Child Poverty (2005) *Key Facts*. Last accessed on 10 March 2005 at: www.ecpc.org.uk/keyfacts.asp

Epstein, J.L. and Saunders, M.G. (2002) 'Family, school and community partnerships', in M.H. Bornstein (ed.), *Handbook of Parenting, Volume 5: Practical Issues in Parenting* (2nd edn), London: Lawrence Erlbaum Associates.

Evans, M. (2004a) 'Mind the gap', *Nursery World*, 3906: 10–11.

Evans, M. (2004b) 'Standing their ground', *Nursery World*, 3919: 10–11.

Every Child Matters (ECM) (2008) *Contact Point Q and A Online*. Last accessed on 6 July 2008 at: www.everychildmatters.gov.uk/_files/ContactPointQandA.pdf

Eyres, I., Cable, C., Hancock, R. and Turner, J. (2004) '"Whoops, I forgot David": children's perceptions of the adults who work in their classrooms', *Early Years*, 24(2): 149–62.

Family and Parenting Institute (2005) *Making Families Matter: Nine Steps to Make Britain Family Friendly*. Last accessed on 1 June 2008 at: *www. familyandparenting.org/Manifesto#3*

Family and Parenting Institute (2008) *About the Fund*. Last accessed on 1 June 2008 at: www.familyandparenting.org/ParentingFundAbout

Featherstone, S. (2004) 'Smooth moves', *Nursery World*, 3919: 14–15.

Fitzgerald, D. (2004) *Parent Partnerships in the Early Years*, London: Continuum.

Fitzgerald, D. and Kay, J. (2008) *Working Together in Children's Services*, Oxford: Routledge.

Frost, N. (2005) *Multi-Agency Teams Working for Children*. Last accessed on 26 February 2005 at: www.rip.org.uk/learningevents/ip_reports/Trusts.asp

Ghate, D. (2001) 'Community-based evaluations in the UK: scientific concerns and practical restraints', *Children and Society*, 15: 23–32.

Gillen, S. (2008) 'Laming: the verdict five years on', *Community Care*, 17 January: 16–17.

Glass, N. (1999) *Origins of the Sure Start Local Programmes*. Last accessed 28 June 2008 at www.surestart.gov.uk/_doc/P0001720.doc

Glass, N. (2001) 'What works for children – the political issues', *Children and Society*, 15(1): 14–20.

References

Goldschmied, E. and Jackson, S. (1994) *People Under Three: Young Children in Day Care*, London: Routledge.

Grisham Brown, J. and Hallam, R. (2004) 'A comprehensive report of child care providers' perceptions of a statewide early care and education initiative', *Child and Youth Care Forum*, 33(1): 19–31.

Hastings, S. (2004) 'Teachers and local Sure Start programmes – their numbers, roles and some issues surrounding their appointment', *Education 3–13*, 32(3): 38–44.

Hennessey, E., Martin, S., Moss, P. and Melhuish, P. (1992) *Children and Day Care: Lessons from Research*, London: Paul Chapman Publishing.

Heywood, C. (2001) *A History of Childhood: Children and Childhood in the West from Medieval to Modern Times*, Cambridge: Polity Press in association with Oxford: Blackwell Publishing.

Hill, A. (2005) 'Childcare shake-up will send men into the nursery', *Observer*, 6 March.

Hill, M. (2000) *Understanding Social Policy* (6th edn), London: Blackwell.

HM Government (2006) *Select Committee for Education and Skills 3rd Report June 2006*. Last accessed on 4th July 2008 at: www.publications. parliament.uk/pa/cm200506/cmselect/cmeduski/478/47802.htm

HM Treasury/Department for Education and Skills/Department for Work and Pensions/Department of Trade and Industry (2004) *Choice for Parents, the Best Start for Children: A Ten-year Strategy for Childcare*, London: HMSO.

Home Office (1998) *Supporting Families: A Consultation Document*, London: HMSO.

Hunter, T. (2005) 'View from the top: teamwork or turf wars?', *Guardian*, 23 February.

Jackson, B. and Jackson, S. (1979) *Childminder: A Study in Action Research*, London: Routledge and Kegan Paul.

Jackson, L. (2005) 'Region rises to the challenge', *Guardian*, 16 February.

Jillian, R. (1996) 'Early years provision in Australia in the 1990s: present status, current issues and future trends', *International Journal of Early Childhood*, 28(1): 48–58.

Jones, C.A. (2004) *Supporting Inclusion in the Early Years*, Maidenhead: Open University Press.

Jones, M. and Lowe, R. (2002) *From Beveridge to Blair: The first fifty years of Britain's Welfare State 1948–98*, Manchester: Manchester University Press.

Joseph Rowntree Foundation (2003) *How Parents Co-ordinate Childcare, Education and Work*. Last accessed on 15 December 2004 at: www.jrf.org.uk/ knowledge/findings/socialpolicy/pdf/593.pdf

Joseph Rowntree Foundation (2005) *Policies Towards Poverty, Inequality and Exclusion since 1997*. Last accessed on 25 March 2005 at: www.jrf.org.uk/knowledge/findings/socialpolicy/0015.asp

Joseph, Sir K. (1975) 'The cycle of disadvantage', in E. Butterworth and R. Holman (eds) *Social Welfare in Modern Britain*, London: Fontana, pp. 387–93.

Kagan, S.L. and Hallmark, L.G. (2001) 'Cultivating leadership in early care and education', *Child Care Information*, 140: 7–10.

Kullas, J. (2000) 'All God's children need to have some space', *Nursery World*, 14 December: 34.

Kurtz, Z. (2003) 'Outcomes for children's health and well-being', *Children and Society*, 17: 173–83.

Laming, Lord H. (2003) *The Victoria Climbié Inquiry: Report of an Inquiry by Lord Laming*, London: HMSO.

Lansdown, G. (2001) 'Children's welfare and children's rights', in P. Foley, J. Roche and S. Tucker (eds), *Children in Society: Contemporary Theory, Policy and Practice*, Basingstoke: Palgrave.

Leissner, A. (1967) *Family Advice Centres*, London: Longman.

Leissner, A. (1972) 'Family advice centres', *Social Work Today*, 2(24): 3–5.

Levin, P. (1997) *Making Social Policy: The Mechanisms of Government and Politics, and How to Investigate Them*, Buckingham: Open University Press.

Levine, R.L. and Fitzgerald, H. (eds) (1992) *Analysis of Dynamic Psychological Systems, Volume 1: Basic Approaches to General Systems Theory and Dynamics Systems, and Cybernetics*, New York: Plenum Press.

Lindon, J. (2005) 'Early stages', *Nursery World*, 3 February.

Lister, R. (2004) *Poverty*, Cambridge: Polity.

Local Government Association (LGA) (2004) *Children Bill and Every Child Matters: Next Steps*, LGA briefing, 5 March 2004. Last accessed on 20 March 2005 at: www.lga.gov.uk/Documents/Briefing/Our_Work/social%20affairs/children.pdf

Makins, V. (1997) *Not Just a Nursery: Multi-agency Early Years Centres in Action*, London: National Children's Bureau.

Marcus, L. (2007) 'Scotland – First Children's Minister', *Nursery World*, 24 May: 4–5.

Masterson, A., Antrobus, S. and Smith, S. (2004) 'The children's national service framework: from policy to practice', *Nursing Management*, 11(6): 12–15.

Melhuish, E. et al. (2005) *National Evaluation of Sure Start (NESS)*, London: Institute for the Study of Children, Families and Social Issues, Birkbeck, University of London.

Mittler, P. (2005) 'The global context of inclusive education: the role of the

United Nations', in D. Mitchell (ed.), *Contextualising Inclusive Education – evaluating old and new international perspectives*, London: Routledge.

Moss, P. (2000) 'Foreign services', *Nursery World*, 3733: 10–13.

Moss, P. (2001a) 'Britain in Europe: fringe or heart?' in G. Pugh (ed.), *Contemporary Issues in the Early Years* (3rd edn), London: Paul Chapman Publishing.

Moss, P. (2001b) 'End of term report', *Nursery World*, 3745: 10–13.

Moss, P. (2003) 'Getting beyond childcare: reflections on recent policy and future possibilities', in J. Brannen, and P. Moss (eds), *Rethinking Children's Care*, Buckingham: Open University Press.

Moss, P. (2004) 'Why we need a well-qualified early childhood workforce', paper presented on 16 March 2004 at Regents College, London.

Muijs, D., Aubrey, C., Harris, A. and Briggs, M. (2004) 'How do they manage? A review of the research on leadership in early childhood', *Journal of Early Childhood Research*, 2(3): 157–69.

Muncey, J. (1988) 'The special school as part of a whole authority approach', in D. Baker and K. Bovair (eds), *Making the Special Schools Ordinary? Vol. 1 Models for the Developing Special School*, London: Falmer Press.

National Audit Office (NAO) (2001) *Modern Policy Making: Ensuring Policies Deliver Value for Money*, London: NAO.

National Audit Office (NAO) (2004) *Early Years: Progress in Developing High Quality Childcare and Early Education Accessible to All*, NAO, HC 268 Session 2003–2004.

National Audit Office (NAO) (2006) *Sure Start Children's Centres*, London: TSO.

National Childminding Association (NCMA) (2005) *The Support Childminder Pathfinder Scheme: Evaluation Report*, London: DFES/Sure Start Unit.

National Children's Homes (NCH) (2003) *United for Children? How Devolution is Impacting upon Children*, London: NCH.

National College School Leadership (NCSL) (2005) *National Professional Qualification in Integrated Centre Leadership Programme* (NPQICL). Last accessed on 30 May 2005 at: www.ncsl.org.uk

National College for School Leadership (NCSL) (2008) *National Professional Qualification for integrated Children's Centre Leadership*. Last accessed on 15 June 2008 at: www.ncsl.org.uk/npqicl-index

National Evaluation of Children's Trusts (NECT) (2004) *Children's Trusts: Developing Integrated Services for Children in England*, Norwich: University of East Anglia/National Children's Bureau/DfES/Department of Health.

National Evaluation of Sure Start (NESS) Research Team (2008) *The Impact of Sure Start Local programmes on Three Year Olds and their Families*, Annesley, Nottingham: DfES Publications. Last accessed on 26 June 2008 at: www.ness.bbk.ac.uk/documents/activities/impact/42.pdf

Nursery World (2001) 'NI children's strategy "could lead the world"' news item in *Nursery World*, 12 July p.6.

Office for National Statistics (ONS) (2003) *Labour Force Survey*, London: ONS.

Office for Standards in Education (Ofsted) (2006a) *Extended Services in Schools and Children's Centres*. Last accessed on 30 June 2008 at: www.ofsted.gov. uk/assets/Internet_Content/Publications_Team/File_attachments/extended2 609.doc

Office for Standards in Education (Ofsted) (2006b) *Inclusion: Does It Matter Where Pupils Are Taught? An Ofsted Report on the Provision and Outcomes in Different Settings for Pupils with Learning Difficulties and Disabilities*. Last accessed on 4 July 2008 at: www.ofsted.gov.uk/publications/ index.cfm?fuseaction=pubs.displayfile&id=4235&type=pdf

Office for Standards in Education (Ofsted) (2006c) *Quarterly Childcare Statistics (30/06/2008)*. Last accessed on 15 June 2008 at: www.ofsted.gov.uk/assets/ Internet_Content/Publications_Team/File_attachments/childstats_jun06.pdf

Office for Standards in Education (Ofsted) (2008) *How Well Are They Doing? The Impact of Children's Centres and Extended Schools*. Last accessed on 30 June 2008 at: www.ofsted.gov.uk/assets/Internet_Content/Shared_Content/Files/ 2008/jan/childcentres_exschs.doc

Organisation for Economic Co-operation and Development (OECD) (2006) *Starting Strong II: Early Childhood Education and Care*, Paris: OECD.

Osgood, J. (2004) 'Time to get down to business? The response of early years practitioners to entrepreneurial approaches to professionalism', *Journal of Early Childhood Research*, 2(1): 5–24.

Patterson, C.J. (2006) Children of Lesbian and Gay Parents, *Current Directions in Psychological Science*, 15(5): 241–4.

Penn, H. (1997) *Comparing Nurseries: Staff and Children in Italy, Spain and the UK*, London: Paul Chapman Publishing.

Penn, H. (ed.) (2000) *Early Childhood Services: Theory, Policy and Practice*, Oxford: Oxford University Press.

Pilkington, C. (2002) *Devolution in Britain Today*, Manchester: Manchester University Press.

Platt, D. (2004) 'The Children Bill and what it means for children's services', paper presented at the Inter-Agency Group Conference, Business Design Centre, London, 15 July. Last accessed 10 June 2005 at: www.csci.org.uk/ about_csci/speches/iag_conference_15)07_04.doc

Pugh, G. (ed.) (1996) *Contemporary Issues in the Early Years: Working Collaboratively for Children* (2nd edn), London: Paul Chapman Publishing.

Pugh, G. (ed.) (2001) *Contemporary Issues in the Early Years: Working Collaboratively for Children* (3rd edn), London: Paul Chapman Publishing.

References

Pugh, G. (ed.) (2006) *Contemporary Issues in the Early Years: Working Collaboratively for Children* (4th edn), London: Paul Chapman Publishing.

Qualifications and Curriculum Authority (QCA) (1999) *Early Years, Education, Childcare and Playwork Sector: A Framework of Nationally Accredited Qualifications*, London: QCA.

Qualifications and Curriculum Authority (QCA) (2004) *The Common Core Prospectus*, London: QCA.

Qualifications and Curriculum Authority/Department for Education and Employment) (QCA/DfEE) (2000) *Investing in Our Future: Curriculum Guidance for the Foundation Stage*, London: QCA and DfEE.

Quinn, G. and Degener, T. (eds) (2002) *The Current Use and Future Potential of United Nations Human Rights Instruments in the Context of Disability*, Geneva: Office of the United Nations High Commissioner on Human Rights.

Rawstrone, A. (2001) 'Scotland provides a good care model' *Nursery World*, 7 June pp. 4–5.

Rickford, F. (2005) '0–19: Do the politicians care?' *0–19*, Comment, 1 March. Last accessed on 9 June 2005 at: www.zero2nineteen.co.uk/Home/default.asp

Roberts, M. (2001) 'Childcare policy', in P. Foley, J. Roche and S. Tucker (eds), *Children in Society: Contemporary Theory, Policy and Practice*, Basingstoke: Palgrave.

Ruxton, S. (2001) 'Towards a "Children's Policy" for the European Union?' in P. Foley, J. Roche and S. Tucker (eds), *Children in Society: Contemporary Theory, Policy and Practice*, Basingstoke: Palgrave.

Sanderson, I. (2003) 'Is it "what works" that matters? Evaluation and evidence-based policy making', *Research Papers in Education*, 18(4): 331–45.

Scottish Executive (2001) *For Scotland's Children*, Edinburgh: Scottish Executive.

Seaton, N. (2006) *Integrated Centres in Wales: Development and Implementation (Final Report)*, Cardiff: Institute of Welsh Affairs.

Senge, P. and Lannon-Kim, C. (1991) *The Systems Thinker Newsletter*, 2 (5).

Sharp, C. (2003) 'School starting age: European policy and recent research', *Early Education*, Spring, pp. 4–5.

Siraj-Blatchford, I. and Sylva, K. (2004) 'Researching pedagogy in English pre-schools', *British Educational Research Journal*, 30(5): 713–30.

Siraj-Blatchford, I., Taggart, B., Sylva, K., Sammons, P. and Melhuish, E. (2008) 'Towards the transformation of practice in early childhood education: the effective provision of preschool education (EPPE) project', *Cambridge Journal of Education*, 38(1): 23–36.

Sheppard, M., MacDonald, P. and Welbourne, P. (2008) 'Service users as gatekeepers in Children's Centres', *Child and Family Social Work*, 13: 61–71.

Shoolbread, A. (2006) *Consulting Children on the proposed Schools (Nutrition and Health Promotion) (Scotland) Bill*, Edinburgh: Scottish Executive.

Skinner, C. (2003) *Running Around in Circles: Coordinating Childcare, Education and Work*, York: Joseph Rowntree Foundation.

Sloper, P. (2004) 'Facilitators and barriers for co-ordinated multi-agency services', *Child: Care, Health and Development*, 30: 571–80.

Smith, C. and Vernon, J. (1994) *Day Nurseries at the Crossroads: Meeting the Childcare Challenge*, London: National Children's Bureau.

Smith, M., Oliver, C. and Barker, S. (1998) *Effectiveness of Early Years Interventions: What Does the Research Tell Us?* Comprehensive Spending Review: Cross-Departmental Review of Provision for Young Children, Vol. 2, London: HM Treasury.

Strategy Unit (2002) *Delivering for Children and Families: Report of the Inter-departmental Childcare Review*, London: Cabinet Office Strategy Unit.

Sure Start (2008) *Districts that Participated in the Mainstreaming Pilot.* Last accessed on 30 June 2008 at: www.surestart.gov.uk/_doc/P0001719.doc

Sure Start Unit (2002) *Birth to Three Matters: A Framework to Support Children in their Earliest Years*, London: DfES.

Sure Start Unit (2003) *Sure Start: Making Life Better for Children, Parents and Communities by Bringing Together Early Education, Childcare, Health and Family Support*, London: DfES Publications.

Sylva, K., Melhuish, E., Sammons, P., Siraj-Blatchford, I. and Taggart, B. (2004) *The Effective Provision of Pre-School Education (EPPE) Project: Findings from Pre-school to end of Key Stage 1*, London: Sure Start.

Teacher Training Agency (2004) *Meeting the Professional Standards: Handbook for Candidates*, London: TTA.

TheyWorkForYou.com (2005). Last accessed on 9 June 2005 at: www.theyworkforyou.com

Tisdall, E.K.M. and Davis, J. (2004) 'Making a difference? Bringing children's and young people's views into policy making', *Children and Society*, 18(2): 131–42.

Tweed, J. (2003) 'One message for reception', *Nursery World*, 3895: 9.

Vimpani, G.V. (2002) 'Sure Start: reflections from down under', *Child: Care, Health and Development*, 28(4): 281–7.

Walker, R. (ed.) (1999) *Popular Welfare for the 21st Century?* Bristol: Policy Press.

Warnock Committee (1978) *Special Educational Needs: The Warnock Report*. London: DES.

References

Warnock. M. (2005) *Special Educational Needs: A New Look.* London: Philosophy of Education Society of Great Britain.

Waterhouse, Sir R. (2000) *Lost in Care: Report of the Tribunal of Inquiry into the Abuse of Children in Care in the Former County Council Areas of Gwynedd and Clwyd since 1974,* London: HMSO (Department of Health).

Waterman, C. and Fowler, J. (2004) *Plain Guide to the Children Act, 2004,* Slough: National Foundation for Educational Research.

Welsh, F. (2002) *The Four Nations: A History of the United Kingdom,* London: HarperCollins.

Welsh Assembly (2004) *Celebrating Progress in Early Years and Primary Education.* Last accessed on 15 November 2004 at: www.learning.wales.gov.uk/scripts/fe/news_details.asp?NewsID=1399

White, G., Swift, J. and Bennett, A. (2005) *Sure Start Mainstreaming Pilots: What Can We Learn?* Annersley: DfES Publications.

Author index

Author index

Subject index

Subject index